Mastering Food Dehydration

© Copyright 2023 by Hector Rend

Copyright © 2023 by Hector Rend
All rights reserved. No part of this book may be reproduced, scanned,
or distributed in any printed or electronic form without permission.

First Edition: November 2023

Cover: Illustration made by Karen L.

Printed in the United States of America

TABLE OF CONTENTS

Dedicated to all my friends and to all the people
who gave me their help.
Thanks a lot
Thanks to all of you for your confidence
in my qualities and what I do.
Hector Rend

CHAPTER 1

UNDERSTANDING FOOD DEHYDRATION

The Science Behind Food Dehydration

Dehydration is one of the oldest, most effective methods of food preservation. By removing moisture, food dehydration inhibits bacterial growth and enzyme activity that lead to spoilage. Understanding the science behind this process allows us to maximize dehydration's benefits.

When drying food, warm circulating air pulls moisture from the food's surface. As surface moisture evaporates, moisture from the interior migrates outward to replace it. This moisture transfer continues as long as conditions enable evaporation. Eventually, moisture content drops low enough that microbial growth and enzyme reactions are minimized.

Three factors affect the rate of moisture removal: temperature, air flow, and humidity. Higher temperatures speed up drying time by increasing the rate of evaporation. Warm air can hold more moisture than cool air, so it pulls moisture from food more quickly. This allows faster moisture migration from the interior to the surface.

Air flow is also critical for carrying away evaporated moisture. The greater the airflow, the faster moisture can be wicked away from the food's surface. Stagnant air would become saturated with moisture, slowing the rate of evaporation. Proper air circulation ensures continuously dry air to absorb surface moisture.

Lower humidity enables faster drying because dry air absorbs moisture better than humid air. The wider the humidity gap between the food's interior and the surrounding air, the higher the moisture migration rate. This is why dry ambient conditions are ideal for dehydration.

As a result of these factors, an environment of warm, dry, moving air creates optimal dehydration conditions. Food dehydrators provide an enclosed chamber for air to efficiently circulate and evaporate moisture.

The effects of dehydration are both physical and chemical. Physically, moisture loss causes foods to shrink and stiffen as water is removed from plant and animal cells. This concentrates flavors and makes the remaining food more compact and shelf-stable.

Chemically, dehydration inhibits spoilage in two key ways - by preventing microbial growth and by slowing enzyme activity. Microorganisms like bacteria, yeasts, and molds require available moisture to grow and multiply. By reducing moisture content sufficiently, usually below 20%, microbial activity is suppressed. Enzymes are also limited without moisture, which slows chemical reactions that lead to ripening, discoloration, and nutrient loss.

Dehydration preserves foods by lowering water activity, a measure of available moisture for bacteria. Foods with low water activity resist spoilage, retaining more nutrients and natural color over long-term storage compared to other methods. Dried foods are less susceptible to damaging oxidative reactions.

Vitamins A, B, and C are particularly prone to loss during heating, hydration, and exposure to air and light. Dehydration uses mild heat for a shorter time than canning or cooking. It better protects these water-soluble vitamins with minimal leaching into water. Antioxidants like polyphenols are also preserved through drying.

By harnessing the science of dehydration, we can efficiently remove moisture to prolong food storage life and retain maximum nutrition and flavor. Understanding these physical and chemical changes allows us to optimize the drying process. With experimentation and observation, anyone can master simple, natural techniques for preserving harvest bounty. Putting science into practice unlocks dehydration as a fun, rewarding way to make the most of fresh foods.

Health Benefits of Dehydrated Foods

Dehydrating food is one of the oldest forms of food preservation, used for centuries to extend the shelf life of foods. By removing moisture, dehydration inhibits the growth of bacteria and molds that cause spoilage. Modern technology has allowed dehydrated foods to become increasingly popular due to their convenience, affordability, and health benefits. Though often associated with highly processed snack foods, dehydrating can be used to create nutritious foods when done properly. This chapter will explore the health benefits of dehydrated foods and how to incorporate more dried fruits, vegetables, meats, and herbs into your diet.

When water is removed from foods through dehydration, the nutrients become more concentrated. Dehydrated fruits like apricots, apples, bananas, and mangos are rich sources of fiber, antioxidants, and phytonutrients. Dried apricots contain high levels of beta-carotene, which the body converts into vitamin A. Just a 1/4 cup provides over 90% of the recommended daily intake for vitamin A. Dehydrated apples are a good source of fiber and polyphenols, which may help regulate blood sugar levels. Banana chips contain resistant starch and magnesium. Mangos are high in antioxidants like quercetin, astragalin, and vitamin C even when dried. Overall, dehydrated fruits make for a healthy alternative to candies and other sugary snacks.

Dehydrated vegetables like tomatoes, carrots, spinach, kale, and mushrooms also pack a nutritional punch. Dried tomatoes contain lycopene, a powerful antioxidant that may lower risk of prostate cancer. Just 28 grams of sun-dried tomatoes provides over 40% of the recommended daily intake of vitamin A. Dehydrated carrots retain their beta-carotene, vitamin K, and potassium. Kale chips are an increasingly popular crunchy snack, providing vitamins A, C, and K. Mushrooms like shiitakes contain immunity-boosting compounds when dried. For hikers and campers, dried vegetables rehydrate easily with water and make lightweight, nutritious additions to trail mix and meals.

Meat jerky and beef sticks have grown in popularity as high-protein snacks. When properly prepared, dried meats can still deliver nutrients like iron, zinc, and B vitamins. Look for products made from lean cuts of beef, which will be lower in saturated fat and calories compared to ones made with fatty ground beef. Turkey, salmon, and other lean meats also make healthy dehydrated options. Try your own homemade jerky using lean grass-fed beef and just a touch of sea salt rather than sugary commercial marinades.

Herbs and spices are perhaps the most common dehydrated ingredients. McCormick, Spice Islands, and other popular brands consist almost entirely of dried herbs like oregano, basil, thyme, rosemary, and parsley. Besides adding flavor, dried herbs deliver antioxidants and medicinal compounds. Oregano contains carvacrol, a natural anti-inflammatory. Rosemary is rich in carnosol, which shows promise for boosting brain health. Daily use of dried basil may help control blood sugar and cholesterol levels. Dehydrated lemon peel contains d-limonene, which gives lemon its cholesterol-lowering benefits.

While dehydrated foods have some advantages over fresh, they do come with a few caveats. The high temperatures used in commercial drying can damage heat-sensitive nutrients like vitamin C. Polyunsaturated fats can also oxidize and become inflammatory during drying. For maximum nutrition, look for brands that use shorter drying times and lower temperatures. Or try making your own dried foods at home with a food dehydrator, which allows more control over the process.

When shopping for dehydrated ingredients, read labels and aim for options with no added sugars, salt, or preservatives. Look for unsulfured fruits preserved without sulfites. Some companies now make vegetable chips seasoned simply with salt and olive oil rather than corn syrup solids and artificial flavors. Be aware that some meat jerkies contain MSG, nitrites, and excess sodium. As with all processed foods, quality can vary widely between brands.

While dehydrated foods make portable, long-lasting options for snacks and emergency supplies, they lack the water content of fresh produce. For overall health, they should not completely replace fresh fruits, veggies, and lean meats. Balance out your diet with primarily whole, minimally processed foods. Think of dried foods as more of a bonus on top of the foundation of your diet. With some discernment in shopping and proper storage, dehydrated foods can be a healthy addition to an already nutrient-rich diet. Their convenience can help increase intake of plant foods and lean proteins. Dehydrating is an age-old preservation technique that, when done right, can create nutritious foods that retain plenty of nutritional value.

In summary, dehydrating foods properly can create nutritious options that are highly portable and long-lasting. When shopping, look for dried fruits, vegetables, herbs, and properly made jerky with short ingredients lists. Balance dried foods as part of an overall nutrient-rich diet for the convenience without over-relying on highly processed options. With some care in preparation and discernment in shopping, dried foods can be an easy way to get more antioxidants, healthy fats, and lean protein in your diet. Dehydrating helps concentrated beneficial compounds in fresh produce and retains many nutrients, though some are still degraded by heating. For food on the go, homemade jerky or dried fruit and nuts make far healthier choices over candy, chips, and other highly processed snacks. With their increased concentration of antioxidants, vitamins, minerals, and fiber, moderate amounts of dried fruits, veggies, herbs, and lean meats can be a wholesome addition to your diet.

The Role of Dehydration in Food Preservation

Dehydration is one of the oldest methods of food preservation, used for centuries to extend the shelf life of foods. By removing moisture, dehydration inhibits bacterial growth and slows down enzymatic reactions that lead to spoilage. Water activity is lowered to a point where microorganisms cannot thrive. With a water activity below 0.85, most foods can be safely stored at room temperature.

Compared to other preservation techniques like canning, freeze drying or irradiation, dehydration has some major advantages. It requires minimal equipment - just a heat source and airflow. The process is energy efficient, using less power to remove moisture than freezing. No preservatives or chemicals are needed. Dehydration causes very little damage to the nutritional value, taste and texture of foods if done properly. Enzymes and vitamins like A and C are retained better than with high-heat methods.

Dehydrated products take up much less storage space, since water weight is reduced by up to 90 percent. They are lightweight, easy to package and convenient for transport. Drying extends the seasonality of fruits, vegetables, herbs and meat, allowing enjoyment of summer produce throughout winter. It allows bulk purchases of seasonal or discounted foods. Home dehydration can save money compared to buying dried, frozen or canned options.

Specific benefits for certain food groups:

Fruits - Dehydration prevents mold growth, browning and fermentation. It halts the activity of ripening enzymes. Dried fruits are high in fiber and minerals. They can be reconstituted for use in various dishes and baked goods. Popular dried fruits include apples, apricots, bananas, cranberries, mangoes and pineapple.

Vegetables - Removal of moisture inhibits the growth of spoilage microorganisms. Shrinking the vegetables cuts down on storage space. Dehydrated veggies like carrots, tomatoes and potatoes are perfect for soups, stews and casseroles. Onions, garlic, mushrooms and peppers add flavor to recipes.

Meats and fish - Dehydration cooks and preserves meats while retaining more nutrients than high-heat canning. Moisture removal inhibits bacterial growth. Dried varieties like beef jerky and shredded fish have a long shelf life. They are light for hiking and camping trips.

Herbs and spices - Dehydration preserves the flavor, color and aroma of herbs and spices. It stops enzymatic activity that causes loss of flavor. Dried basil, oregano, parsley, chili peppers and more can add taste to any dish. No need for freezing or refrigeration.

Beyond food preservation, dehydration offers other practical benefits:

Crafts - Fruits like oranges and apples can be dried for fragrant, decorative wreaths and potpourri. Kids will love making dried fruit leather. Mix powdered cornstarch and herbs for scented bath salts.

Potpourri - Many flowers and herbs hold their scent beautifully when dried. Lavender, rosemary, lemon balm and more can be combined for custom potpourri.

Medicine - Dehydration preserves and concentrates the natural chemical compounds of medicinal herbs. It's an ancient method for making chamomile, echinacea, calendula, ginger root and other remedies.

Botanicals - Drying prepares delicate flowers, herbs and plants for use in crafts and displays. Retaining color and shape, they can be used to make wreaths, pressed flowers and more.

While traditional air or oven drying are most common for home use, large-scale food manufacturing employs other methods:

Freeze drying - Also known as lyophilization, this vacuum process pulls moisture directly from frozen foods. It better preserves crispness, aroma and nutrition. Used for instant coffee, dried fruit, spices, ready meals and more.

Spray drying - Food liquids are atomized into a hot gas system to evaporate moisture nearly instantly. Used for dairy powders, coffee, juices and other liquids.

Drum drying - Involves drying on heated metal drums to produce sheets of dried product. Used for potato flakes, milk powder, mashed vegetable flakes and more.

While industrial techniques allow mass production, the basic principle remains the same. By efficiently removing water, dehydration enables foods to stay edible much longer than their fresh counterparts. It creates lightweight, easily stored products that provide nutrition and flavor long after harvest season is over. Home drying requires minimal investment and provides satisfying DIY options. As an energy-efficient method with little detriment to food quality, dehydration is likely to remain an important preservation technique for centuries to come.

In summary, dehydration powerfully inhibits microbial growth and spoilage enzymes to extend shelf life. It requires only simple equipment, retains nutrients better than high-heat methods, needs no preservatives and reduces storage space needs. Drying enables enjoyment of seasonal produce year-round, bulk buying savings and lighter loads for travel. Beyond food preservation, dehydration preserves flowers, herbs and materials for crafts and displays. While air drying works for homes, methods like freeze drying and drum drying enable mass production. Yet all leverage dehydration's efficacy in removing moisture to prevent spoilage. As a versatile, natural preservation technique, dehydrating foods will continue nourishing people far into the future.

Dehydration for Busy Individuals and Families

In today's fast-paced world, finding time to prepare healthy meals can be a challenge for busy households. Dehydrating food is an efficient way for time-strapped families to make the most of fresh ingredients. Dried foods offer a quick, nutritious solution for hectic schedules.

Dehydrating food in batches saves time compared to daily cooking. Preparation and active drying may take a few hours, but it yields multiple servings of shelf-stable ingredients. These can be rehydrated and incorporated into meals throughout the week. With a little planning, dried items like vegetables, herbs, and pre-cooked meals can be your go-to ingredients for fast weeknight dinners or brown bag lunches.

Dried foods are ideal grab-and-go options for breakfasts, snacks, and lunches on the run. Home-dried fruits, veggie chips, and jerky offer wholesome alternatives to processed snack foods. They provide nutritious energy to fuel kids' active lifestyles and keep adults going during busy workdays.

Rehydrating dried ingredients is faster than cooking from scratch. Soaking dried beans, chopping rehydrated veggies, or combining dried soup mixes with hot water cuts meal prep time significantly. Advance preparation means assembling healthy meals in minutes when time is scarce.

Take advantage of seasonal or bulk purchases by dehydrating surplus produce. When neighborhood trees deliver bountiful harvests or you spot a great sale, drying lets you capture that seasonal goodness year-round. Excess garden vegetables and berries become pantry staples rather than waste.

For dishes like stews, soups, and sauces, prepare a large batch, then dehydrate portions in advance. Later, just add water and serve homemade "fast food" in minutes. Make extra to set aside dried herbs, vegetables, and pre-cooked meats.

Dehydrating reduces grocery costs by preserving homegrown and purchased foods at their nutrient-rich peak. The homemade versions cost a fraction of commercially dried products. Enjoy premium quality and ingredients while saving money.

Kids can help with washing and slicing fruits and veggies for the dehydrator, instilling good eating habits. Let them create their own personalized snacks by choosing fun combinations. Drying's visual magic captures kids' curiosity as foods transform.

Tap the potential of an extra appliance already in your kitchen. Use the oven or toaster oven to dehydrate small batches. Or explore compact electric models that tuck onto a counter corner.

Monitor the dehydrator's progress periodically rather than standing over a hot stove. Simple to operate, most run safely unattended for hours. Multi-tray models maximize each drying session.

Dried foods help streamline meal planning and preparation. Make a master list of your go-to items so they're always on hand. Store pre-made mixes in jars for quick cooking. Pull from your pantry of dried ingredients to throw together no-fuss family meals.

Harnessing dehydration helps today's busy families reduce food waste, save money, and gain flexibility. Turn seasonal abundance into fast, wholesome meals and snacks all year. Dehydrating makes it easy to provide quality nourishment despite your hectic schedule. Rediscover the value of creating simple, wholesome foods together as a family.

Dehydration for Outdoor Adventures and Emergency Preparedness

Dehydrated foods offer a number of benefits for outdoor adventurers and those preparing for emergencies. When water is removed from foods through dehydration, the resulting dehydrated items become lightweight, compact, and easy to transport. This makes them ideal for backpacking trips, camping excursions, and storing in emergency kits. In this chapter, we will explore the advantages of using dehydrated foods for outdoor and emergency situations.

To begin, dehydrated foods are extremely lightweight compared to their non-dehydrated counterparts. The removal of water content reduces the overall weight and bulk of the food. For hikers, campers, and other outdoor enthusiasts who need to carefully monitor the weight of gear in their packs, this is a major advantage. Dehydrated foods allow them to carry nutritious meals without being burdened by excessive weight. For emergency kits, the lightness of dehydrated foods enables people to store a greater quantity and variety without their kits becoming too large or heavy.

In addition to being lightweight, dehydrated foods take up very little space. Their low moisture content allows them to become tightly compressed, taking up a fraction of the volume of their original form. This compactness makes dehydrated foods easy to tuck into crowded backpacks and emergency kits. Outdoor adventurers can carry more calories in a smaller space, ensuring they have enough sustenance for lengthy trips. For emergency preparedness, the compact size means entire meals can be tucked into tight storage areas for grabbed quickly when needed.

The compressed nature of dehydrated foods also makes them less prone to spoilage. Their lack of moisture content inhibits bacterial growth and slows the spoilage process. This gives dehydrated foods a longer shelf life than their hydrated counterparts, even without refrigeration or special packaging. The extended shelf life enables outdoor enthusiasts to prepare food supplies well in advance of a trip without worrying about perishability. For emergency kits, it alleviates concerns about having to frequently rotate supplies to avoid spoilage. Dehydrated foods can be stored for months at a time if kept in proper conditions.

When it comes time to eat dehydrated foods, they can be easily rehydrated by adding hot water. This allows for warm, comforting meals even when cooking facilities are limited. For backpackers, a pot of hot water is all that's needed to transform dehydrated ingredients into satisfying soups, stews, and more. For emergency situations, the ability to make a hot meal with minimal resources is invaluable for providing comfort during stressful times. The rehydration process also allows the foods to regain much of their original texture and volume. With the addition of water, dehydrated items can rehydrate to closely mimic their non-dehydrated versions.

Some examples of dehydrated foods that are ideal for outdoor and emergency use include:

- **Dehydrated fruits and vegetables** - These retain much of their nutritional value and can provide healthful supplements to unbalanced diets common during trips or emergencies. They are lightweight, compact, and great for snacking.

- **Dehydrated meats** - Meat jerky and shredded meat bars help satisfy protein needs in lightweight, durable forms. They provide high energy and nutrition.

- **Dehydrated eggs** - Dehydrated scrambled egg mix allows for protein-rich morning meals with just hot water. The rehydrated eggs resemble fresh scrambled eggs.

- **Dehydrated dairy** - Powdered milk and butter provide essential nutrients and can be used to make oatmeal, hot cereals, sauces, and more while camping or during an emergency.

- **Dehydrated meal kits -** Pre-made meals like chili, stew, pasta, or rice dishes allow for fast preparation with minimal effort or supplies. They are compact, lightweight, and great for emergencies when cooking resources are scarce.

- **Dehydrated baking mixes -** Carrying ready-to-use pancake, muffin, or bread mixes allows for fresh, warm baked goods that provide comfort during outdoor trips or emergencies. Just add water or oil and cook over a fire or stove.

- **Dehydrated soup mixes -** Carrying bouillon cubes or powdered broths allows for nourishing, filling soups by just adding hot water. Soups are comforting, convenient meals for outdoor or emergency settings.

With their long shelf life, light weight, compact size, and easy reconstitution, dehydrated foods are clearly well-suited for outdoor adventure and emergency preparedness situations. They allow for nutritious, satisfying meals to be carried and consumed even when space, weight, and cooking resources are extremely limited. Whether planning for a long backpacking excursion or stocking supplies for an emergency kit, including an array of dehydrated foods is recommended. Just be sure to account for sufficient water and cooking supplies to properly rehydrate the foods when it comes time to eat. With the right resources, dehydrated foods can form the basis of meals that sustain energy and morale even in the most remote or challenging situations. For outdoor and emergency food needs, dehydrated is truly ideal.

CHAPTER 2

GETTING STARTED WITH FOOD DEHYDRATION

Choosing the Right Dehydrator

Selecting the right dehydrator is key to successful food dehydration. With options ranging from basic models under $50 to premium machines over $500, it can get confusing to determine what best suits your needs and budget. This chapter will guide you through the key factors to consider when investing in a food dehydrator.

There are two main types of dehydrators: stackable and box. Stackable dehydrators have trays that slide into a tower unit. Box or cabinet style have a solid outer box and internal drying chamber. Stackables maximize drying space, while box models offer more consistent temperatures.

Within these types, your choice comes down to factors like:

Capacity - Consider how much you plan to dehydrate at one time. Small 1-2 tray models work well for herbs and jerky. Medium 4-6 tray models easily handle fruit leathers and veggies. For large batches, 10+ tray stackables or 9-12 square foot box models excel. Expandable dehydrators allow adding more trays later.

Temperature range and adjustment - Look for a range encompassing 95°F to 160°F for optimal flexibility with different foods. Adjustability in 5-10 degree increments allows customizing for each food.

Airflow - Models with rear mounted fans and horizontal airflow provide the most efficient moisture removal. Box types often offer better airflow than stackable.

Expandability - As your dehydration skills grow, you may want to dry larger batches. Expandable dehydrators allow adding trays later by simply stacking more.

Timer and shutoff - Timers from 30 minutes up to 48 hours automate the process for perfect results every time. Auto shutoff turns the dehydrator off when done.

Materials - Plastic or metal trays withstand high temperatures. Stainless steel resists staining. BPA-free plastic is better for foods prone to sticking.

Special features like temperature probes, fruit roll sheets, and herb drying attachments allow customizing as you advance. Consider your budget and how frequently you plan to use the dehydrator. Here are top picks in different price ranges:

Under $50 - Affordable for casual users. Lacks extras but efficiently dries foods. Great for starter batches.

- Presto Dehydro Electric Food Dehydrator ~$40

- Nesco FD-37A ~$45

- MAGIC MILL Professional Dehydrator ~$50

$50-$150 – Ideal balance of price and features for regular use. More drying space and options.

- Excalibur 3926TB ~$150

- Nesco FD-60 Snackmaster ~$70

- Chefman 6-Tray Food Dehydrator ~$60

Over $200 – Advanced models for enthusiasts. Offer premium materials, large capacity, and versatile features.

- Excalibur 9-Tray Electric Dehydrator ~$250

- Tribest Sedona Express SDE-S6780 ~$260

- COSORI Premium Food Dehydrator ~$160

While fancier models offer specialized features, basic electric dehydrators are suitable for most home drying needs. Here are tips for picking the right affordably-priced model in the $50 to $100 range:

- Seek 4-6 BPA-free plastic trays for flexibility.

- Look for 500 to 700 watts of drying power.

- Opt for 95°F to 160°F temperature range.

- Choose adjustable thermostats in 5-10 degree increments.

- Seek horizontal airflow for efficient moisture removal.

- Get a timer offering up to 48 hours continuous runtime.

- Seek dishwasher-safe trays for easy cleaning.

- Find a model with overheat protection and auto shutoff.

- Choose stackable trays for expandable capacity.

- Seek a 12 to 24-hour timer and adjustable thermostat.

- Make sure the dehydrator is ETL certified for safety.

- Look for a model with a drip tray to catch juices.

- Seek a one-year warranty from a reputable brand.

With a good mid-priced dehydrator, you can dry fruits, vegetables, meats, herbs and more with consistent, quality results. While compact models are fine for starters, those serious about dehydration will benefit from more drying space. Carefully compare ratings and reviews before deciding.

By choosing the right dehydrator for your needs, you will be on your way to enjoying the many benefits of food dehydration. With the guidance in this chapter, you can find the model with the right balance of affordability, capacity and functionality that best suits your situation. Soon you'll be making healthy dried snacks, creating fruit leathers and crafting flavorful spice blends thanks to your properly outfitted dehydrator.

Preparing Foods for Dehydration

Proper preparation is key to successfully dehydrating foods. Taking a little extra time upfront to prep your ingredients correctly will ensure the best results.

Start by selecting high-quality, fresh foods at the peak of ripeness. Produce with bruises or blemishes can be trimmed, but avoid using anything overly ripe or spoiled. The best candidates for dehydration retain good texture, vibrant color, and robust flavor when dried.

Wash all foods thoroughly before prepping to remove dirt, chemicals, or microbes. Scrub firm fruits and vegetables with a brush under running water. Clean herbs by swishing leaves in a bowl of cool water. For mushrooms, wipe caps with a damp cloth rather than soaking.

Pat foods very dry before cutting to prevent dilution of flavors. Wet surfaces won't dehydrate efficiently. Use paper towels or a salad spinner for leafy herbs and greens.

Cut pieces uniformly for even drying. Aim for consistent thickness no more than 1/4 to 1/2 inch. Slice fruits and veggies into coins, strips, or small cubes. Halve or quarter larger fruits like apples. Leave grapes, cranberries, and cherry tomatoes whole.

Keep an eye on food safety when working with meats, fish, and poultry. Use clean tools and surfaces. Cut into thin strips or small cubes to speed drying. Partially freeze meats first for easier slicing.

Pre-treat certain fruits and veggies to prevent browning or improve texture. Soak sliced apples and pears in acidulated water made with lemon juice or citric acid. Blanch broccoli, green beans, and asparagus by briefly boiling then cooling in ice water to stop cooking.

For herbs and leafy greens, remove any thick, tough stems that take longer to dry. Pull thyme or rosemary leaves off woody stems before drying the leaves whole. Remove kale or chard ribs and stems before drying the tender leaves.

Other vegetables may also benefit from peeling or coring first. Peel waxy skins from onions, shallots, garlic, carrots, or beets. Core seeded vegetables like tomatoes or bell peppers. Peel and deseed winter squashes.

Leaving skins on many fruits and some veggies adds nutritional value and fiber. Apples, pears, peaches, plums, nectarines, apricots, and grapes dry well unpeeled. Simply wash the skins before slicing.

Pre-cooking or blanching denser vegetables helps them dry more evenly. Boil carrots, sweet potatoes, cauliflower, turnips, or winter squash briefly before dehydrating.

Consider pre-freezing berries like strawberries and blueberries before drying. Freezing ruptures cell walls, allowing moisture to escape faster during dehydration.

For herbs and garlic, chopping or mincing after drying intensifies flavors. Wait to mince onion and chives until ready to use to retain texture.

Proper prep sets the stage for success. Taking time upfront to wash, peel, trim, cut, pretreat, and blanch your foods enables even drying and great results. Follow these guidelines as you prep your next batch of ingredients for dehydrating.

Understanding Dehydration Times and Temperatures

When dehydrating foods, one of the most important factors to control is the temperature and time required to sufficiently remove moisture. Finding the right balance of temperature and time serves multiple purposes. It ensures food safety by achieving the proper internal temperature to kill pathogens. It also prevents over-drying, which can cause undesirable texture changes, nutrient loss, or spoilage. In this chapter, we'll explore optimal time and temperature guidelines for dehydrating various foods.

To start, it's important to understand how temperature impacts the dehydration process. Higher temperatures cause moisture to evaporate more rapidly. However, excessively high temperatures can also "cook" the exterior of food before the interior is dried. This leaves the inside under-dehydrated while creating hardened exteriors. Moderately high temperatures between 130-155°F are typically recommended, as these facilitate thorough drying without overcooking. Within this range, specific temperatures should be selected based on the characteristics of the food being dehydrated.

Fruits and vegetables with high water content require relatively long dehydration times at moderate temperatures. The extra time allows moisture to fully evaporate from their porous structure without heat damage. 130°F is suitable for most fruits, while 140°F works well for most vegetables. Some examples include:

- Sliced apples: 6-15 hours at 130°F

- Strawberry slices: 8-20 hours at 130°F

- Broccoli florets: 8-14 hours at 140°F

- Sweet bell pepper slices: 6-12 hours at 140°F

Leafy greens and herbs dry more quickly and are prone to heat damage, so lower temperatures around 110-125°F are best. Drying times range from 4-8 hours. For example:

- Kale leaves: 4-6 hours at 115°F

- Basil leaves: 4-6 hours at 120°F

Meats require precise temperature control to ensure safety. Temperatures of at least 145°F must be maintained to eliminate bacterial growth. Poultry should be dried at 160°F and red meats at 155°F. The additional heat helps meat dry efficiently in shorter time spans of 4-8 hours.

For fruits and some vegetables, pretreatments can shorten dehydration time. Soaking in acidified water, sugar syrup blanching, or steam blanching prior to dehydrating can accelerate moisture removal. This reduces overall drying time by up to 25-50% for some foods. For example, pretreating apples slices before dehydrating at 130°F reduces drying time from 15 hours to about 6-8 hours.

The form and size that foods are cut into also impacts dehydration time. Smaller pieces have more surface area exposed for moisture to evaporate, speeding drying. Thin slices or dices of fruit and vegetables dehydrate more quickly than larger chunks or whole produce. Meats should be sliced no more than 1/4 inch thick for efficient moisture removal. Even shreds or crumbles dry faster than meat chunks.

Water activity, or the availability of moisture that supports bacterial growth, is a technical indicator of doneness. Most dehydrated foods are adequately preserved when their water activity is reduced to around 0.60 to 0.70. Checking water activity requires special equipment, but this target is generally achieved by following the above temperature guidelines for each food type.

Lastly, the initial moisture content affects the length of dehydration. Foods that naturally contain more water, like tomatoes (94% water) and watermelon (92% water), require longer drying than drier items like potatoes (79% water). Be mindful that drying times are estimates, and food should be checked for doneness rather than relying solely on elapsed time.

In summary, key factors impacting dehydration time and temperature include:

- Type of food - Fruits, vegetables, meats

- Structure and size of pieces

- Pretreatments - Blanching, sulfur dioxide, etc.

- Temperature used - Higher temps speed drying

- Initial moisture content

By understanding how these elements interplay, you can determine the best approaches for your specific foods. Monitor doneness through texture tests rather than only time. Fruits and veggies should have no moist spots. Meats should be leathery yet brittle. With the right balance of time, temp, and testing, you can achieve great quality dehydrated foods that are safe and shelf-stable.

Safety Tips for Food Dehydration

Dehydrating food at home provides many benefits, but it's important to follow key safety practices to avoid any potential health risks. By understanding proper sanitation, storage, rehydration and cooking guidelines, you can ensure your dried foods retain nutrients, flavor and textures while remaining safe to eat.

Start with high quality ingredients free of bruises, damage or mold. Wash fruits and vegetables thoroughly. Trim meats of excess fat and freeze for 30 minutes before dehydrating to kill any parasites. Blanching is recommended for vegetables, helping destroy harmful enzymes and microbes prior to dehydrating. Steam blanch for 3-5 minutes or boil for 1 minute, then quickly dry and cool before dehydrating.

Sanitize dehydrator trays in hot, soapy water or the dishwasher. Wipe the base unit down with appliance cleaner or diluted vinegar. Wash hands thoroughly before and during prep. Try marinating produce in lemon, orange, pineapple or grapefruit juice for additional antimicrobial effects.

Use proper temperatures to ensure safety. Meat, poultry, fish and vegetables should be dried at 140-160°F to quickly pass through the "danger zone" of 40-140°F where bacteria can rapidly multiply. Hold fruits at 130°F or lower to prevent loss of enzymes, vitamins and antioxidants. Herbs do best at 95-115°F.

Monitor food closely as it dehydrates. Discard any pieces that appear discolored or smell unpleasant. Check for visible moisture and doneness. Cut thicker foods may need flipping during dehydration to evenly dry.

Let foods cool fully before testing for dryness. Conditioning returns moisture evenly and allows resting the food. Place dried items in sealed containers for 1-2 weeks, shaking daily, then reheat at 145°F for 15 minutes before final storage.

Packages should be moisture- and vapor-proof. Glass jars, freezable plastic bags and vacuum seal bags work well. Oxygen absorbers or desiccants can help remove trace oxygen and moisture. Store in cool, dark places. Refrigeration or freezing gives longest shelf life.

Rehydrate dried food in potable water either by soaking or simmering until tender. Discard any unused rehydrating liquid. Bring soups and stews with rehydrated ingredients to a full boil before serving. Rehydrated meats should reach 165°F internally.

Safe prep tips by food category:

- **Fruits** - Pretreat to prevent browning. Use clean produce free of mold. Dehydrate citrus peels thoroughly until crisp.

- **Veggies** - Blanch or partially cook Dense vegetables before dehydrating. Discard any moldy or mushy pieces.

- **Meats** - Freeze first to control bacteria. Use lean cuts and blot excess fat. Discard if any spoilage is present.

- **Fish** - Freeze first for safety. Dehydrate fillets, jerky strips or hand-flaked chunks fully. Grill or boil rehydrated fish.

- **Herbs** - Ensure excellent air circulation. Discard any deteriorated leaves. Store away from light and moisture.

Some key takeaways to remember:

- Inspect ingredients and discard anything spoiled

- Wash produce thoroughly before use

- Blanch vegetables before dehydrating

- Use proper temperature settings for each food

- Allow foods to fully cool before testing dryness

- Condition dried items for 1-2 weeks before final storage

- Use moisture-proof packaging and cool storage

- Rehydrate safely and cook reused liquid to 165°F

- Bring rehydrated meats and fish to safe serving temperatures

By following these tips, you can safely enjoy your home-dehydrated foods for months to come. Take time to process ingredients, sanitize equipment, maintain optimal temperatures and practice proper storage. The rewards will be nutritious, economic homemade snacks and meals your whole family can savor while staying healthy.

Dehydration opens a world of healthy snacking opportunities. With an array of dried fruits, vegetables, herbs and jerky on hand, you can avoid vending machine snacks and enjoy natural, wholesome foods even while traveling or camping. Vacuum sealed veggies make instant backpacking meals by just adding hot water.

Preserve your garden's bounty for year-round enjoyment by dehydrating seasonal fruits and produce at their flavor peak. Make big batches when your favorite fruits are cheap at the farmer's market. With proper sanitation and storage, dried foods can retain nutrients for over a year.

Reduce food waste in your household by dehydrating leftovers, overripe produce and meat trimmings. Powdered vegetable dregs add nutrition to soups and smoothies instead of rotting in the trash. Revive stale bread, pastries and cookies by dehydrating them into crunchy croutons or crumbs.

Dehydration allows expanding your culinary horizons with new textures and concentrated flavors. Use dried mushrooms, tomatoes, peppers and berries to add complexity to recipes. Make your own fragrant potpourris and crafting materials from flowers and herbs.

As you advance your dehydration skills, continue following the core safety principles in this chapter. Eat the safest, most nutritious dried foods by starting with quality ingredients and using proper sanitation, blanching, drying and storage methods.

Tips for Dehydration Success

Mastering the art of food dehydration takes experimentation and patience. Follow these tips gathered from experienced dehydrators to help ensure success on your drying adventures.

Know your dehydrator. Read the instruction manual to understand its key features and optimal operation. Look for information on temperature ranges, airflow, and humidity controls. Learn how trays and accessories such as fruit leather screens work. Start by following any pre-set programs or manufacturer guidelines for various foods.

Record details for each batch. Date your dried items and make notes on drying temperatures, times, and observations for future reference. This helps you fine tune methods for specific fruits, vegetables, herbs, and meats over time.

Start small. Don't overwhelm your machine or your learning curve. Run one or two test trays with different foods to begin. As you gain experience, scale up to larger batches.

Rotate trays and shuffle food occasionally for even drying. Move trays from top to bottom shelves and shuffle individual pieces around during drying. This exposes all sides to air flow.

Don't overload trays. Allow space between pieces so air can circulate freely. Cut back batch sizes if needed.

Watch closely near the end. Check food and tester pieces more frequently as items near dryness. The last stage often progresses quickly. Don't over-dry foods past the target moisture level.

Use the power of your senses. Observe, touch, taste, smell. Let your eyes, fingers, taste buds, and nose guide you. They detect signs of readiness long before moisture meters.

Test doneness before removing trays. Let pieces cool briefly before checking to avoid burns. Bend to test leathery texture. Taste a cooled tester piece to verify flavor concentration.

Handle with care. Dried items are fragile when removing trays. Use spatulas and gentle handling to avoid crushing or breaking.

Allow proper cooling before storage. Let pieces cool thoroughly before placing in airtight containers. Trapped internal heat causes condensation and invites mold.

Use best storage practices. Store in glass jars, vacuum seal bags, or opaque plastic containers. Label and date everything. Keep in a cool, dry, dark place.

Condition herbs and chillies. Place them uncovered in the refrigerator 24-48 hours post-drying to distribute remaining moisture evenly before sealing in airtight containers.

Learn from mistakes. Don't get discouraged by dried fruits that are overly leathery or hard vegetables. Analyze what went wrong and adjust for next time.

Expect variations. Drying times fluctuate with humidity, the season, and produce quality. Your experience guides adjustments.

Focus on food safety. Use clean tools, wash produce, and monitor temperatures carefully when drying meat, poultry or fish.

Keep a drying journal. Note drying times, temperatures, observations, and adjustments batch by batch. This accumulates knowledge over seasons and years.

Practice patience. Some items like leathery fruits and dense vegetables can take 36 hours or longer. Resist temptation to hurry the process.

Follow your instincts. After fundamentals are understood, have confidence to experiment based on your observations and preferences.

Relax and enjoy the process. Approaching dehydration with curiosity and flexibility maximizes rewards. Drying intensifies nature's bounty into delicious, nutritious treasures.

CHAPTER 3

DEHYDRATING FRUITS AND VEGETABLES

Best Practices for Dehydrating Fruits

Dehydrating brings out the vibrant flavors and chewy textures of favorite fruits transformed into satisfying, nutritious snacks or wholesome ingredients. Follow these best practices for success with all your favorites.

Select ripe, fresh specimens at their flavor peak. Fully ripe fruit concentrates sugars, acids, and aromas during drying. Tree-ripened local varieties hold up better than grocery store fruit bred for transport and shelf life.

Wash thoroughly. Use cool running water to rinse away any dirt, chemicals, or microbes. Scrub skins of firm fruits gently with a vegetable brush. Halve fruit and scoop out cores or pits before slicing to expose more surface area for faster drying.

Pre-treat. To prevent browning, soak light-colored fruits in acidulated water - 1 tbsp lemon juice or powdered citric acid per cup of water. Alternatively, blanch 1-2 minutes in boiling water. Use leaner blanching for berries.

Prepare uniformly sized pieces. Aim for 1/4 inch slices, halves, cubes, or strips to promote even drying. Leave small berries, grapes, or cherry tomatoes whole. Cut apples, pears, peaches, plums, mangoes, pineapple, etc. into coins.

Arrange in single layers, no overlapping. Allow ample space between pieces for air circulation to speed drying.

Dry at 130-140°F until pliable and leathery. Pineapple, mango, banana, apple, and pear take 6-12 hours. Berries may only need 6-8 hours. Monitor closely near the end.

Condition dried fruit before jarring. Let pieces sit out loosely covered for 7-10 days to redistribute moisture. Some moisture loss occurs during conditioning.

Check for doneness. Bend a piece in half - it should not break. Berries should have no visible moisture and rattle when shaken in a jar. Conditioned fruits will be slightly more pliable.

Past the leathery stage, fruits become too dry and turn dark. If too stiff or brittle, they were over-dried. Excessive drying removes volatile flavor compounds.

After cooling completely, promptly store in airtight glass jars or freezer bags. Press out excess air and seal. Label and date. Refrigerate berries and tropical fruits; store apples, peaches, plums at room temperature. Enjoy dried fruit within one year for best flavor, texture and nutrition.

Rehydrating restores some moisture before eating dried fruit. Steam or simmer in water or juice until pliable but still chewy. Best for use in cereals, baked goods, trail mixes.

Try creative fruit combos like Strawberry-Rhubarb, Blueberry-Orange, or Peach-Ginger. Lightly coat dried fruit in dark chocolate for a sweet treat. Mix with nuts and seeds for homemade trail mix.

Dehydrating creates a concentrated burst of flavor and nutrition from fresh seasonal fruits. Follow these guidelines to create delicious dried fruits your family will crave.

Recipes for Dehydrated Fruits

Dehydrated fruits open up a world of possibilities when it comes to recipes and meal prep. Taking fresh fruits and removing the moisture condenses the flavors and nutrients into portable, shelf-stable ingredients. Dehydrated fruits are versatile and can be used in a wide variety of dishes, from breakfasts to desserts and everything in between. In this chapter, we'll explore some of the many ways to incorporate dehydrated fruits into delicious recipes.

To begin with breakfast, one simple way to use dehydrated fruits is blending them into smoothies. Dried fruits add natural sweetness and nutrients, providing an energy boost first thing in the morning. Bananas, strawberries, mangos and pineapple all make great additions. Start with a base of milk or yogurt, then add a cup of your favorite dehydrated fruits. Blend until smooth for a refreshing and filling start to the day.

Another breakfast idea is to mix dehydrated fruits into oatmeal or cereal. The dried fruits plump up in the hot cereal and add wonderful flavor contrast. Dried apples, cranberries, raisins, apricots and prunes pair especially nicely with classic oatmeal. Get creative with mix-ins like pumpkin seeds, cinnamon and nutmeg for a customized fruit and grain bowl.

Dehydrated fruits also make easy on-the-go snacks. Simply toss some dried mango, pineapple, banana chips or apple rings into small baggies or containers. The concentrated sweetness curbs cravings and provides an energy boost at school, work or on adventures. For variety, make DIY trail mixes with nuts, seeds and whole grain cereal to create satisfying homemade snack medleys.

At lunchtime, liven up greens or grain salads with diced dried fruits. Their sweet tanginess balances nicely against bitter greens like kale or arugula. Cantaloupe, strawberries and blueberries are all suitable options. For grain-based salads, add raisins, cranberries or apricots to quinoa or couscous for a flavor pop. Dried fruits also make wholesome sandwich or wrap fillings paired with nut butters or cheese for contrast.

For appetizers, dried fruit and nut combinations always make a crowd-pleasing choice. Create colorful platters with dried apricots, figs, dates, plums and more accompanied by roasted nuts or seeds. The natural sugars caramelize and become concentrated during dehydration, creating delicious complexity. Arrange dried fruits and nuts on skewers or platters for easy finger foods to enjoy before dinner.

Dehydrated fruits also shine in both savory and sweet main dishes. To add texture and flavor to savory entrees like rice dishes, stirred fries or roasted vegetables, sprinkle on some diced mango, pineapple, papaya or cranberries during the last few minutes of cooking. The fruits plump up while lending pop of color and natural sweetness. For more traditional fruit-based dishes, use dried apples, pears or apricots as the basis for tarts, galettes, crumbles and other desserts. Rehydrate them first for a tender filling.

Finally, dehydrated fruits offer the perfect finishing touch on yogurt parfaits and sweet casual desserts. Top yogurt or ice cream with diced peaches, pineapple, banana chips and other textures. Mix into no-bake energy bites, granola bars or chilled chia puddings. The options are endless for adding dried fruits to create simple yet satisfying sweet treats.

Some tips when cooking with dehydrated fruits:

- Rehydrate in hot water or juice before adding to dishes if a less chewy texture is desired.

- Use scissors to snip larger dried fruits into smaller pieces for easier inclusion into recipes.

- Reduce any added sugars in recipes since dried fruits offer natural sweetness.

- Experiment with ingredient pairings and preparation methods to prevent dried fruits from becoming overly tough when cooked.

With their concentrated flavors and versatility, dehydrated fruits are valued additions in the kitchen. Whether used in appetizers, main dishes or sweet treats, they provide a nutrition boost while adding color and intrigue. If you have an abundance of dried fruits, get creative and see how many recipes you can enhance with their sweet, chewy goodness. Your breakfasts, lunches, dinners and snacks will never be the same.

Best Practices for Dehydrating Vegetables

Dehydrating is an excellent way to preserve vegetables at their nutritional and flavor peak. By following some best practices, you can maximize quality while ensuring safety. Proper pretreatment, temperature control and storage will reward you with nutritious dried veggies to enjoy any time of year.

Start by selecting prime vegetables free of blemishes, bruises or mold. Choose produce in season for highest quality. Farmers markets and home gardens offer great ingredient sourcing. Varieties naturally higher in sugars and acids like carrots, peppers, tomatoes and mushrooms dry best. Starchy veggies like potatoes need pretreatment.

Wash all vegetables thoroughly before dehydration. Peel waxy skins if desired. Proper cleaning removes debris and surface microbes. Soak in diluted white vinegar or potassium metabisulfite solution for extra sanitation.

Pretreating vegetables prior to dehydrating improves texture, flavor and safety. Blanching halts enzyme actions to prevent loss of color and nutrients. It helps remove surface microbial populations and initiates softening of fibers.

Steam blanch veggies by placing in a steamer basket for 3 to 5 minutes. Boil for 1 minute for leaves, pods and delicate produce. For thicker produce, use longer steam times from 5 to 8 minutes. Shock immediately in ice water to stop cooking.

Pre-cooking converts the starch in low-acid veggies like potatoes, sweet potatoes, beets, parsnips and white carrots to simpler sugars, improving their stability in storage. Simmer pieces in hot water, microwave until partially tender or roast in the oven before dehydrating.

Enzyme pretreatments like lemon juice, pineapple juice and honey help prevent browning of light colored fruits and vegetables by blocking enzyme activity. Dip or spray cut surfaces with juices or commercial anti-browning preparations.

Drying temperatures significantly impact final vitamin content. Lower temperatures around 110-125°F maximize retention of heat-sensitive vitamins like vitamins C and A. For herbs and greens, 100°F works well.

Faster drying at 140-160°F better preserves bright colors and flavors. Higher temperatures minimize risks of mold growth. Meat and poultry should be dried at 160°F minimum to ensure safety.

Monitor progress regularly. Evaluate thickness and moisture content as vegetables dehydrate. Rotate trays and shuffle pieces as needed to ensure even drying. Turn thicker vegetables like sweet potato slices periodically.

Test dried vegetables for readiness when leathery with no moisture inside. Condition by storing in sealed containers for 1-2 weeks to redistribute remaining moisture. Then use finished veggies promptly or pasteurize and repackage for extended storage.

Vacuum packaging, freezer bags and glass jars all safely preserve dehydrated vegetables. Oxygen absorbers and desiccants help remove trace oxygen and moisture. Store in a cool, dark place for longest shelf life. Refrigerate or freeze for multi-year storage capacity.

Rehydrating returns vegetables to a tender, moist texture. Place pieces in soups, stews or boil until fully restored. Avoid over-soaking to prevent dilution of nutrients and flavor. Discard any excess liquid after vegetables are rehydrated.

Follow these tips when dehydrating common vegetables:

- Corn - Blanch kernels 2 minutes before drying to 145°F.

- Mushrooms - Clean thoroughly, slice uniformly and dry at 90-100°F until crispy.

- Peppers - Core and seed bell peppers before dehydrating at 125°F until leathery.

- Greens - Blanch leaves 1 minute then dry at 90-100°F until brittle.

- Carrots - Clean, peel, thinly slice and steam blanch 3 minutes before dehydrating.

- Tomatoes - Blanch or roast quarters until softened before drying at 130-140°F.

- Potatoes - Parboil or bake slices before dehydrating thoroughly at 130-140°F.

With careful pretreatment, temperature control and storage, dried vegetables retain nutrition for extended use. Follow best practices to maximize quality and safety. Soon you'll have a pantry stocked with wholesome dried veggies to add convenience and flavor to meals throughout the year.

Dehydrating during seasonal bumper crops allows enjoying produce year-round. Make big batches of dried vegetables when prices drop at late summer's peak. With proper sanitation, pretreatment and storage, dried veggies can offer nutrients for over a year after harvest.

Preserve your garden's bounty at its flavor and nutrition height. Halt ripening, browning and molding by quickly dehydrating abundant vegetables following best practices. Enjoy bright flavors and colors long after the growing season ends.

Reduce food waste by dehydrating leftovers and overstock before they spoil. Powder older vegetables to add extra nutrition to soups, stews and smoothies. Dehydrate stalks, peelings and ends for veggie stock rather than trashing them.

Dehydration condenses flavors and brings out natural sweetness in many vegetables. Intensify tastes in cooked dishes by rehydrating veggie powders or using dried mushroom pieces. Make crunchy low-calorie snacks by seasoning and drying kale, okra or bean chips.

Follow the guidelines in this chapter to maximize quality and safety with all your dehydrated vegetables. With proper techniques, you can create a nutritious, natural pantry full of garden-fresh flavor to nourish your family in any season.

Recipes for Dehydrated Vegetables

Transform fresh vegetables into crispy, flavor-packed dried ingredients to enjoy as nutritious snacks or instant additions to meals with these tasty recipes.

Homemade Vegetable Chips

Thinly slice vegetables like carrots, sweet potatoes, beets, parsnips, or jicama. Optionally blanch slices first. Arrange in single layers on dehydrator trays. Dry at 125°F for 6-10 hours until crispy. Flip once halfway through. Enjoy as crunchy snacks or salad toppers.

Variations:

- Root Veggie Chip Mix - Combine sliced carrots, sweet potatoes, beets, parsnips

- Tropical Veggie Chips - Try plantain, taro root, cassava, malanga

- Italian Veggie Chips - Slice zucchini, eggplant, bell peppers, artichokes

- Herbed Veggie Chips - Toss slices with dried herbs before dehydrating

Fruit and Veggie Leathers

Puree your choice of vegetables, fresh or cooked. Sweeten if desired. Spread puree 1/4 inch thick onto dehydrator fruit leather trays. Dry at 135°F for 4-8 hours until no sticky wet spots remain. Peel from tray while still warm before rolling up. Rehydrate in soups or stews.

Flavor combos:

- Tomato-Basil, Roasted Red Pepper, Butternut Squash, Carrot-Ginger, Sweet Potato-Cinnamon

Dehydrated Onion and Garlic

Peel, slice, and dry yellow, red, or sweet onions at 125°F for 6-10 hours until very brittle. Allow to cool completely before crushing or powdering in a blender or with a mortar and pestle to maximize flavor. Store powered onions in an airtight container.

Follow the same process for garlic cloves. Peel before slicing thinly. Dry until shriveled and brittle. Crumble into powder once fully dried.

Vegetable Seasoning Mix

Combine equal parts crumbled dried onion, garlic powder, dried celery flakes, dried bell pepper flakes, dried parsley, and optional dried tomato powder. Store in an airtight container. Sprinkle on meats, eggs, pasta, roasted vegetables, popcorn. Use to liven up soups, stews, and sauces.

Homemade Sun-dried Tomatoes

Slice Roma tomatoes about 1/4 inch thick. Optionally salt lightly. Arrange in single layers on dehydrator trays. Dry at 135°F for 6-10 hours until leathery. Pack in oil or freeze for storage. Enjoy on pizzas, pastas, sandwiches, salads.

Make the most of your garden's bounty with these easy recipes for crisp vegetable chips, concentrated fruit and veggie leathers, pungent onion and garlic powders, flavorful herb mixes, and succulent sun-dried tomatoes.

Storing and Rehydrating Your Dried Fruits and Vegetables

Proper storage and rehydration help maximize flavor, texture, and nutrition of your home-dried produce. Follow these guidelines to get the most from your dehydrated fruits and veggies.

Storage Tips

Cool completely before packaging. Ensure pieces reach room temperature to avoid condensation from trapped heat.

Use sealing containers. Glass canning jars, Mylar bags, and vacuum seal pouches prevent oxygen and moisture from compromising dried food. Opaque plastic containers also work well.

Exclude air. Press out oxygen, seal lids tightly, and use vacuum sealers when possible. Oxygen accelerates enzymatic activity and vitamin degradation.

Keep in cool, dark place. Store in the refrigerator, basement, or other spot with low, stable temperatures around 60°F. Darkness prevents vitamin destruction.

Limit storage time. For best flavor and nutrition, enjoy dried produce within one year. Properly stored in cool, dark, airtight conditions, most fruits and veggies last 1-2 years.

Label containers. Mark contents and date packages. Rotate stock by using oldest products first. Discard anything moldy, stale, or deteriorated.

Freeze for long-term storage. For storage beyond a year, place dried food in sealed freezer bags or containers. Keeps items viable for 2-5 years at 0°F.

Rehydration Methods

Steaming. Place dried food in steamer basket over boiling water. Cover and steam until pliable. Good for fruits.

Simmering. Add dried food to saucepan with small amount of water or juice. Simmer over low heat until softened. Better for vegetables.

Soaking. Place dried items in bowl and cover completely with warm or room temperature water. Soak 30 minutes to 4 hours. Works for most fruits, veggies, beans.

Microwaving. Add dried food to microwave-safe dish and add enough water to cover. Microwave in 30 second increments, allow to sit 1-2 minutes before checking softness. Avoid overcooking.

Rehydration Tips

- Add seasonings into soaking or cooking liquid for more flavor

- Strain and save excess soaking liquid for soups, stews, gravies

- Drain fully before adding rehydrated items to recipes to avoid diluting dishes

- Pat off excess moisture before eating or adding to salads

- Allow longer soak and cook times for dense vegetables and beans

- Test texture frequently to avoid over-softening

With good storage practices and proper rehydration techniques, your dried garden and orchard bounty can nourish you and your family with optimal nutrition and bright flavors for many seasons to come.

CHAPTER 4

DEHYDRATING MEATS AND FISH

Preparing Meats and Fish for Dehydration

Properly preparing meats and fish prior to dehydrating is an important step to ensure safety, quality, and long-term storage. Taking the time to trim, pretreat, and slice or cut meats and fish enables them to dehydrate fully and evenly. Following best practices also eliminates bacteria that can cause spoilage or foodborne illness. In this chapter, we'll review techniques for preparing beef, poultry, pork, and fish to set them up for successful dehydration.

For beef, select lean cuts like flank steak, sirloin tip, or 95% lean ground beef. Excess fat can turn rancid over time. Trim off any thick sections of visible fat. Partially freeze the meat for 30-60 minutes to make slicing easier. Cut into 1/4 inch strips or thin slices across the grain of the meat. This short muscle fiber length helps the meat rehydrate faster later on.

Poultry also benefits from trimming prior to dehydrating. Remove any excess skin or fat from chicken, turkey, or other birds. Leaving skin on can result in greasy dried meat. Slice chicken breast across the grain into 1/4 inch strips. For whole cuts like thighs or drumsticks, debone then slice into thin pieces.

For pork, choose lean cuts like loin or tenderloin. Trim any fat cap to prevent rancidity over time. Partially freezing makes slicing easier. Cut pork across the grain into 1/4 inch strips or slices for even drying. Ground pork can also be dehydrated after being shaped into thin patties. Cure raw pork using a salt-based mixture before dehydrating to control bacteria like salmonella.

Fish is best when very fresh before dehydrating. Rinse fillets under cold water and pat dry with paper towels. Trim off any excess fat or connective tissue. Slice fish no more than 1/4 inch thick, with 1/8 inch being optimal for very dense fish like salmon. Cutting across the grain helps fish flakes rehydrate better later.

Pretreating meats and fish is recommended prior to dehydrating. For beef and poultry, marinating in acids like lemon juice, vinegar, yogurt or wine for 30-90 minutes helps kill surface bacteria. Salt, sugar, and phosphate mixtures also help curb microbial growth in meats. Fish benefits from a salt brine for 30 minutes to an hour before dehydrating.

In addition to pretreatments, proper meat dehydration temperature is vital. Use a thermometer to ensure the internal temperature reaches 145°F for whole cuts of beef, pork, and lamb. 165°F is safest for ground meats. Poultry should reach an internal temp of 165°F, and fish between 130-140°F. This eliminates pathogens and enzymes that speed spoilage.

Some additional tips for best results include:

- Pat all pieces completely dry before loading trays to maximize dehydration efficiency.

- Lay pieces in a single layer without overlapping or touching to enable air flow on all sides.

- Rotate trays and stir pieces periodically to ensure even drying.

- If needed, cut thicker pieces in half after partially dried to expose moist interiors.

- Check for doneness by looking for leathery texture with no moist spots.

Properly preparing meats and fish truly sets the stage for effective dehydration. Follow these best practices, and you'll end up with delicious jerkies, biltongs, dried salmon, and more that are both long-lasting and safe to enjoy. Always remember to handle raw proteins carefully and maintain proper sanitation. With the right prep, you can avoid bacteria issues and yield shelf-stable dehydrated proteins to savor any time.

Best Practices for Dehydrating Meats

Dehydrating is a safe, effective way to preserve meats while retaining maximum nutrition and flavor. Follow these best practices for selecting, preparing and drying various types of meat. Proper temperatures, curing and storage will reward you with delicious jerkies, biltongs and dried meats to enjoy anytime.

Always start with high-quality, fresh raw meats. Choose lean cuts with minimal fat content. Venison, beef, chicken, turkey and fish all dehydrate well. Meat should be chilled at 40°F or frozen at 0°F prior to use. Freeze meat for 30 minutes before dehydrating to kill any potential parasites.

Trim off all visible fat, which can turn rancid and cause spoilage. Cut meats across the grain in thin, uniform slices to enable fast drying. Partially freeze meat to make slicing easier. Cut width depends on preferences, but 1/8" thick or less works well.

Marinating meats prior to dehydrating adds big flavor. Use acidic ingredients like citrus, wine, vinegar and yogurt to tenderize meats and help prevent bacterial growth. Oil-based marinades enhance texture but can hasten rancidity. Refrigerate marinated meats for up to 24 hours.

Curing meats beforehand improves safety and preservation. Salt curing dehydrates the surface. Use a dry cure of 1 tbsp salt per 1 lb meat along with herbs, spices and sweeteners if desired. Refrigerate 1-7 days until firm. Rinse cured meat before dehydrating.

Set dehydrator temperatures between 145-160°F to quickly dry meats. Higher heat shrinks meat fibers, forcing out moisture. Temperatures below 130°F may allow bacterial growth. Most meats take 6-15 hours to fully dehydrate.

Rotate trays and shuffle pieces periodically for even drying. Blot up any beads of oil or moisture during dehydration. Check meats often near the end to prevent case hardening. Condition in sealed containers 1-2 week to redistribute moisture.

Test for dryness by examining internal color and texture. Meat should be firm but not brittle. There should be no moist spots. Conditioned meats can be pasteurized in a 175°F oven for 10-15 minutes before final storage.

Vacuum packaging, freezer bags and mason jars all help preserve dehydrated meats. Oxygen absorbers and desiccants prevent moisture and off flavors. Store in the refrigerator or freezer for best retention of quality and safety.

Before eating, rehydrate dried meats by simmering in stew, gravy or broth until tender and heated through to 165°F internally. Avoid over-soaking to prevent dilution of the meat's flavor. Discard any leftover rehydration liquid after cooking.

Here are some meat-specific tips:

- **Beef** - Choose lean cuts like flank steak. Cut across the grain before marinating and dehydrating.

- **Chicken** - Remove skin and dehydrate seasoned breast meat cut into thin strips.

- **Turkey** - Breast meat works best. Slice thinner than beef due to milder flavor.

- **Pork** - Opt for loin or tenderloin, trimming fat. Marinate before drying into jerky strips.

- **Fish -** Cut into 1/4" chunks or strips after freezing. Dehydrate oily fish lightly smoked or salted.

Following proper handling, prep and dehydration guidelines results in flavorful, tender dried meats. With the right techniques, you can use your dehydrator to create a protein-packed pantry ready to enjoy anytime.

Dehydrating surplus garden vegetables allows enjoying their nutrients year-round. Blanch or juice them first to maximize retention of heat-sensitive vitamins. With the right pretreatments, temperatures and storage, dried vegetables offer flavors and nutrition for over a year after harvest.

Preserve your garden's bounty at its peak flavor and nutrition. Halt ripening and degradation by quickly dehydrating vegetables following best practices. Enjoy bright flavors and colors long after the growing season ends.

Reduce food waste by dehydrating abundant veggies before they spoil. Powder older vegetables to add extra nutrition to soups, stews and smoothies. Dehydrate stalks, peels and ends for stock rather than trashing them.

Intensify vegetable flavors through dehydration. Condense flavors and bring out natural sweetness in many vegetables. Use rehydrated veggie powders or dried mushrooms to add complexity to dishes. Make crunchy low-calorie snacks by seasoning and drying veggie chips.

Follow the guidelines in this chapter to maximize quality and safety for all your dehydrated vegetables. With proper techniques, you can create a nutritious, garden-fresh pantry to nourish your family any time of year.

Recipes for Dehydrated Meats

Dehydrating is a safe, effective way to preserve meat's nutrition and bold flavors condensed into portable, protein-packed snacks and ingredients. Here are flavorful recipes to make the most of your dried meats.

Homemade Beef Jerky

Slice lean beef into 1/4 inch thick strips. Trim any fat which can turn rancid. Marinate 1-2 hours in your favorite jerky seasoning or marinade like soy sauce, Worcestershire, liquid smoke, brown sugar, spices. Pat very dry. Arrange strips in a single layer on dehydrator trays, without touching or overlapping. Dry at 145-155°F for 4-8 hours until leathery with no moisture inside. Cool completely before storage.

Turkey and Salmon Jerky Variations: Use boneless turkey breast or salmon filets sliced 1/4 inch thick. Adjust marinades to complement the flavors. Dry turkey at 145°F for 4-6 hours until firm but pliable. Dry salmon at 130°F for 6-8 hours until opaque and dry to touch.

Homemade Pemmican

Traditional pemmican combines dried lean meat with rendered animal fat. Grind dried beef, venison, or bison into a coarse meal using a blender or food processor. Add just enough melted beef tallow, lard, or other rendered fat to coat the dried meat and form into a paste. Optionally incorporate dried berries and spices. Form mixture into bars and wrap individually in wax paper, then store in sealed bags in a cool location.

Campfire Stew Mix

Combine equal parts crushed dehydrated potatoes, carrots, peas, corn, green beans, and chopped dried chicken or beef. Season with onion powder, garlic powder, salt, and pepper. At camp, add mix to pot with water and simmer until vegetables are tender. Quick and hearty.

Meat Biltong

Originally from South Africa, biltong is dried, spiced meat similar to jerky but not smoked or cooked. Slice beef, game meats, or poultry thinly across the grain. Soak briefly in vinegar. Coat pieces with spices like coriander, pepper, salt, brown sugar. Air dry for 2-3 days until ready to chew but slightly moist in center.

With an array of global flavors and endless combinations, dehydrating allows you to make delicious, wholesome meat products to enjoy anywhere.

Best Practices for Dehydrating Fish

Dehydrating fish enables you to preserve the flavors and nutrition of fresh catches for long-term enjoyment. When done properly, the process concentrates the savory umami taste into portable, shelf-stable dried fish. However, dehydrating this delicate protein does require care and the right techniques. Follow these best practices for prepping, dehydrating, and storing dried fish to achieve quality results.

To start, select only the freshest fish possible for dehydrating. Fish begins deteriorating immediately after catching, so start the drying process as soon as you can. If freezing fish prior to dehydrating, do so quickly using a blast freezer and thaw just before use. Oily fish with high moisture like salmon and tuna are best candidates for dehydration. Lean fish can become too dry and hard.

Once you have fresh fish in hand, begin prepping by filleting and skinning the flesh. Slice fillets against the grain into 1/8 inch thick pieces. Thinner slices mean faster and more even drying. Weigh down the pieces as you work to keep them flat. Next, dip the fish briefly in citrus juice, vinegar or wine. These acidic marinades "cook" the surface proteins, killing bacteria. Pat the slices thoroughly dry.

Arrange fish slices in a single layer on dehydrator trays without overlapping. Air flow around each piece is crucial. To prevent sticking, line trays with parchment paper or silicone mats. Temperature and time will vary based on factors like slice thickness, but aim to dehydrate at 130-155°F for 4-8 hours. Fish dries quickly, so check periodically to avoid over-drying.

Rotate trays and shuffle pieces at least once mid-way through dehydration to ensure uniform results. Check thickness and moisture content of pieces. Thicker parts may need more time. Dried fish should be brittle yet flexible when cool. If needed, cut partially dried pieces in half to expose moist interiors for further drying.

Before storing, pasteurize dried fish to eliminate any lingering bacteria. Place pieces in an oven or dehydrator at 145°F for 10 minutes, then 165°F for 30 minutes more. Finally, condition the dried fish for a week in sealed jars out of direct light. This equalizes moisture and allows the fibers to relax. Enjoy immediately or store in a cool, dark place up to one month. Refrigerate or freeze for longer storage.

When preparing your homemade dried fish, keep these tips in mind:

- Work quickly with very fresh, sushi-grade fish. Discard any questionable pieces.

- Cut uniform, thin slices and lay flat without overlapping on trays.

- Dry at 130-155°F up to 8 hours, checking frequently to prevent over-drying.

- Rotate trays and shuffle pieces midway for even results. Cut thicker pieces.

- Pasteurize finished fish before conditioning in sealed jars for one week.

- Enjoy immediately or store properly refrigerated or frozen.

Follow these best practices starting from the quality of your fish through storage, and you'll be rewarded with delicious dried fish full of concentrated flavor. Experiment with spices and marinades to customize your creations. Just be sure to handle raw fish safely and sanitize all prep tools. With the right care, you can create amazing homemade dried fish to enjoy for months to come. From salmon to snapper, the possibilities are bountiful.

Recipes for Dehydrated Fish

Dehydrated fish offers a tasty and healthy pantry staple, easy to take camping or keep on hand for quick meals. This chapter shares flavorful recipes for preparing and cooking with dried fish. Get inspired to use your dehydrator's capabilities for making seafood soups, dips, snacks and more.

A key advantage of dehydrated fish is convenience. Complex prep work like skinning, deboning and slicing is done in advance. The concentrated flavors and textures make delicious meals by just rehydrating and seasoning the pieces. Vacuum-sealed pouches keep dehydrated fish safely preserved for years.

Compared to fresh fish's short shelf life, dried fish offers extended enjoyment and less waste. It also avoids concerns about contaminants like mercury in larger predator fish. Smaller fish like sardines, anchovies, herring and smelt work wonderfully for dehydrating. Their omega-3 fatty acids survive drying.

Experiment with herbs, spices, citrus and other acids when marinating fish before dehydrating. Consider flavors that will complement the finished dish. Garlic, onions, pepper, lemon and wine make excellent marinades. Allow pieces to soak up seasoning for a few hours in the refrigerator before drying.

Salmon jerky offers a nutritious snack to take hiking or keep in your purse or desk drawer. Mix soy sauce, brown sugar, ginger and garlic to marinate skinless salmon chunks or strips before dehydrating 6-12 hours until glossy and dry.

Smoked salmon jerky has even deeper flavor. First lightly smoke skinless salmon pieces for 1-2 hours until lightly golden and firm. Then dehydrate until dried. The touch of smoke complements the concentrated salmon essence beautifully.

For an easy feast, rehydrate your dried fish pieces by simmering in pasta sauce, enchilada sauce, coconut milk or curry. Serve over rice or baked potatoes. The fish's intensified flavor infuses the entire dish. Garnish with fresh herbs and lemon.

Turn fish pieces into creamy chowders or hearty stews. Simply rehydrate them by simmering for 15-20 minutes in broth, milk or a combo. Season with onions, potatoes, corn and spices. Purée some of the mix for a thick, velvety texture.

For an elegant appetizer, make rillettes by whipping rehydrated fish with butter or olive oil, lemon, shallots and herbs. Chill the spread overnight to allow flavors to meld. Serve with crackers or crusty bread.

Combine dried fish bits with mayonnaise, sour cream, Greek yogurt or avocado for an easy sandwich filling, dip or spread. Jazz it up with capers, onion, minced pickles or olives. Serve crackers, cut veggies or rustic bread.

Make your own Caesar dressing by puréeing rehydrated anchovies or sardines with olive oil, lemon juice, garlic, Parmesan, egg yolk and seasonings. Toss with shredded romaine and croutons for a classic salad.

For a protein power snack, simply rehydrate fish pieces in plain water. Alternatively, boil with soy sauce, sesame oil and chili paste for Asian-inspired flavors. Sprinkle with sesame seeds and serve room temperature.

Whirl rehydrated fish with beans, garlic and olive oil for an instant flavor-loaded bean dip. Add hot sauce and cumin for a southwestern twist. Garnish with chopped tomato, green onion and cheese.

Simmer dried shrimp or small fish in coconut milk with aromatic ingredients like lemongrass, ginger, garlic, chilies and a dash of fish sauce. Toss with rice noodles or serve over jasmine rice.

The options for cooking with dehydrated fish are nearly endless. Make Mediterranean meals with olives, tomatoes, wine and oregano. Opt for Indian flavors like turmeric, cumin and coriander. Enjoy Nordic inspiration with dill, mustard and potatoes. Simply rehydrate and combine with your favorite ingredients and seasonings.

With the recipes and ideas in this chapter, you can fully utilize your dehydrator to make delicious dried fish dishes. Bring the flavors of the sea wherever you roam and cut meal prep time with conveniently preserved fish. Get ready to enjoy healthy, tender seafood meals and snacks even when landlocked or on the go.

CHAPTER 5

DEHYDRATING HERBS AND SPICES

Benefits of Dehydrating Herbs and Spices

Drying allows us to preserve herbs' fresh flavors and spices' potent aromas long after the growing season ends. Harnessing their concentrated essences is rewarding and economical.

Intensified Flavor

The drying process removes moisture yet retains volatile aromatic oils, greatly intensifying herbs and spices' tastes and smells. Slow evaporation condenses the compounds that provide robust flavor and fragrance.

Dried parsley, oregano, sage, thyme, and other herbs burst with brightness ideal for rubs, marinades, dressings, and sauces. Dehydrated cloves, cinnamon, nutmeg, ginger, and peppers pack a powerful punch perfect for baking and simmering in stews. Their flavors carry well beyond fresh.

Convenience

Drying provides flavors of fresh herbs and ground spices on-demand, long after harvest. Having them already prepped and shelf-stable saves grocery store trips. Just reach for your homegrown dried seasonings any time a dish needs a flavor boost.

Storage and Shelf Life

Proper storage protects dried herbs and spices for 1-2 years or longer. Sealed glass jars in a cool cupboard or freezer bags in the freezer help retain volatile oils that dissipate over time, prolonging flavor. No need to use while fresh - dried is there when you need it.

Versatility

Dried herbs and spices lend versatility to all types of cuisine. Italian, Mexican, Indian, French, Middle Eastern dishes all rely on dried seasonings. Garlic, onion, basil, cumin, clove, cinnamon - these ingredients traverse food cultures. Home drying lets you customize.

Nutrition

Drying preserves much of herbs' nutritional value - vitamins A and C, antioxidants, and phytochemicals that benefit health. Using dried herbs generously boosts nutrition in your cooking.

Food Safety

Drying inhibits microbial growth by removing moisture. And unlike freezing, it halts enzyme activity that causes loss of flavor, color, texture. Drying is a low-temperature process preserving delicate flavors and aromas lost at high heats.

Quality

You control the ingredients and process when home drying herbs and spices. No added preservatives, artificial flavors, colors, or anti-caking agents like many commercial brands use. Just pure, natural flavor from herbs nurtured in your garden and spices sourced in bulk.

Cost Savings

Purchasing fresh bunches of herbs and bulk bags of dried spices can get expensive. Grow your own herbs and dry a surplus. Buy larger bags of spices and preserve remainders by drying the excess. Saving money is satisfying.

Creativity

Makesignature seasoningblends andspice mixes for uniqueflavor profiles. Experiment with global spice combinations.Create homemade gifts personalized withyour own herb and spice blends.

Herb and spice drying unlocks a world of flavorful possibility, nutrition, and convenience that brightens soups, stews, meats, vegetables, breads, desserts, and more.

Preparing and Dehydrating Herbs and Spices

Drying fresh herbs and spices allows you to preserve their flavor and aroma long-term for enhanced home cooking. When harvested and dehydrated properly, herbs and spices retain their volatile oils and other compounds that imbue dishes with delicious complexity. This chapter will explore best practices for selecting, prepping, and dehydrating a variety of common herbs and spices.

When choosing herbs for drying, it's important to start with prime specimens at their peak. For leafy herbs like parsley, cilantro, basil and mint, look for vibrant colors and perky leaves without wilting or discoloration. Pick woody herbs like rosemary, thyme and oregano just as their flower buds form for maximum potency. The same goes for seeds like dill and fennel—choose plants with robust seed heads. Dig roots like ginger and turmeric when the leaves and stems above ground start to yellow and die back.

Prep leafy herbs by first sorting leaves and discarding any that are damaged, discolored or flowering. Rinse briefly under cool water and shake dry. Smaller leaves can be left whole to dry intact. For larger leaves, strip them from their stems before drying. Woody herbs can be dried on their stems if small enough or stripped from stems like leafy herbs if larger.

Proper sanitation prevents mold growth during the extended drying process. Wash all equipment and surfaces first. Maintain temperatures of at least 95°F and air circulation to inhibit microbial growth. Enclose drying spaces from insects that can contaminate the herbs and spices. Low humidity around 25% is also optimal to facilitate moisture evaporation.

When loading herbs and spices for dehydration, avoid overcrowding. Arrange in single layers to enable airflow all around. Set temperatures between 95-115°F and dry most herbs for 1-4 hours, checking frequently. Delicate leaves and flowers dry in 1-2 hours while thick roots may take up to 8 hours. Monitor until crisply dry but still aromatic.

Condition dried herbs after dehydration by letting them mellow in sealed containers for 1-2 weeks. This redistributes internal moisture. To kill any lingering mold spores, pasteurize delicate leafy herbs at 120°F for 30 minutes or longer if in larger batches. Heartier herbs, seeds and roots only need 10 minutes.

Proper storage prevents flavor and quality loss over time. For short term storage up to six months, keep dried herbs in air-tight containers out of direct light. Refrigeration extends shelf life to one year for most herbs, while the freezer preserves quality for several years.

Below are some specific tips for select herbs:

- Basil: Choose small leaves. Dry whole or chiffonade sliced at 95°F for 1 hour.

- Oregano: Dry on stems up to 4 hours at 110°F. Crumble leaves after drying.

- Rosemary: Strip leaves from stems before drying. Dry 2 hours at 105°F.

- Bay leaves: Pat leaves clean but don't wash before drying. Dry 12 hours at 95°F.

- Ginger: Peel and slice root thinly before drying up to 8 hours at 105°F.

- Garlic: Clean but don't peel cloves. Slice thinly before drying at 100°F for 6 hours.

With the right selection, prep, drying, and storage, you can stock your own kitchen with amazing dried herbs and spices. Your cooking will benefit all year from the concentrated flavors and aromas. Adjust techniques as needed for your specific plant varieties and growing conditions. In no time, you'll be enhancing dishes with your own homemade dried herbs and spices.

Recipes Using Dehydrated Herbs and Spices

Dried herbs and spices are pantry powerhouses, infusing dishes with bold flavor. This chapter shares tips and recipes for cooking with dehydrated herbs and spice blends. Bring new life to everyday meals by amplifying flavors with your own homemade dried seasonings.

One major benefit of dehydrating herbs and spices is intensified flavor and aroma. Removing moisture distills down the plant oils and compounds that give herbs their characteristic tastes and scents. Simply mince rehydrated herbs before adding them to dishes.

Start by dehydrating herbs like basil, oregano, rosemary, thyme, sage, parsley, cilantro, dill, mint and more. Chop leaves finely and dry on trays at 95°F until crisp. To use, just crumble the dried herbs into sauces, soups, roasted vegetables and anything needing fresh herbal taste.

Likewise, dry minced garlic, onion, shallots, ginger, lemongrass and hot peppers. Store in shakers to instantly flavor dishes. Rehydrate in a little warm water first for maximum impact if the pieces are large. They pack a flavor punch.

To make spice blends, dehydrate individual spices like cumin, coriander, cinnamon sticks, cardamom, cloves, bay leaves, mustard seeds, fennel and peppercorns. Use a coffee grinder to powder them. Mix your own signature combos.

Customize blends to various cuisines. Indian mixes may contain cumin, turmeric, coriander, cinnamon, clove, cardamom, chili powder, curry leaves and black pepper. Italian mixes incorporate basil, oregano, rosemary, red pepper flakes, garlic and onion.

To craft seasoning blends, combine dried herbs, spices, garlic, onion and salt. Think about flavor profiles and adjust ratios to preference. Make barbecue rubs, poultry seasoning, chili powder mixes and more.

Bring out the unique flavors of various proteins by making your own marinades and rubs using dried ingredients. Massage spice rubs into meats before grilling. Marinate chicken or fish using pastes made from garlic, ginger, chilies and oil.

Whip up flavored salts and sugars by drying and grinding herbs, citrus peels or floral ingredients like lavender or rose petals. Use to rim glasses, season meat and desserts, or sweeten tea.

Replace store-bought broths and bouillon with homemade versions. Simmer vegetable scraps and bones with dried onions, garlic, herbs and spices to create rich, nourishing stock.

Make your own tea blends with dried fruits, herbs, flowers and spices. Customize soothing herbal teas, spicy chai mixes or fruity iced tea combos. Brew into a comforting hot drink or refreshing infusion.

Transform simple vegetables like carrots, green beans, cauliflower or potatoes by roasting them tossed in oil and dried herbs like rosemary, thyme and oregano. The herbs permeate the vegetable's flavor.

Stir dried herbs and spices into olive oil to infuse it with their essence. After several weeks the oil will be saturated with herbal notes perfect for dipping bread or dressing salads.

The possibilities are endless when cooking with your own dehydrated seasonings. Make weeknight dinners more exciting by spicing up basic recipes. Share the gift of flavor with friends by packaging your own blends, rubs and salt mixes into jars.

Storing Dehydrated Herbs and Spices

Proper storage is key to preserving the flavors and aromas of dried herbs and spices. Follow these tips for maximizing shelf life and quality.

Cool, Dark Location

Store containers in a cool, dark cupboard or pantry. Light, heat, and humidity cause herbs and spices to lose volatile oils, diminishing flavor. An ideal storage temperature is 60-65°F. For long-term storage exceeding one year, the freezer maintains quality.

Airtight Containers

Choose glass, plastic, or metal containers that seal tightly. Glass canning jars work well. Opaque plastic or stainless steel helps block light. The goal is an airtight environment that prevents air and moisture from entering. Vacuum sealed bags or containers are ideal.

Limit Air Exposure

When first filling containers, press down on dried herbs and spices to compact them and force out air before sealing lids. For vacuum bags, opt for the medium to heavy duty thickness. The less air remaining inside, the better.

Water-resistant Container

If storing in the freezer, choose containers safe for freezing temperatures to avoid cracks. Glass jars may break. Use freezer-grade plastic bags or rigid plastic containers instead.

Smaller Containers

Storing dried herbs and spices in smaller containers that hold 1-4 ounces minimizes air exposure each time you open and take what you need. Open large bags or jars only when refilling your everyday use containers.

No Refilling

Never add new dried herbs or spices to a container that already has some product in it. This introduces moisture and compromises the remaining contents. Always start fresh in an empty container.

Label Contents

Clearly label each container with the herb or spice name and year packaged. This lets you easily rotate stock by using oldest first, and identify mystery jars years later.

Monitor Condition

Inspect inventory occasionally. Check for moisture, mold, or signs of deterioration. Discard anything questionable. Dried herbs and spices kept over 2 years will slowly decline in potency.

Proper storage requires a little thought, but pays off in preserved flavor and shelf life. Follow these tips to keep your dried herbs and spices fresh and potent for 1-2 years of robust flavor in your dishes.

Rehydrating Your Herbs and Spices

Bringing dehydrated herbs and spices back to life with rehydration opens up endless possibilities for enhancing foods with homegrown flavors. By returning moisture to dried plant matter, you can reconstitute herbs and spices to use just like fresh. With the right techniques, rehydrated herbs and spices infuse recipes with nuanced taste and vibrancy. In this chapter, we'll explore best practices for unlocking the full potential of your dried aromatic ingredients.

To start, assess the state of your dehydrated herbs. If stored improperly or for too long, they may have lost volatile oils that are difficult to restore via rehydration. But herbs and spices kept no more than 6-12 months in cool, dark, airtight spaces should rehydrate well. Squeeze a small pinch. Brittleness is ideal. Leathery, rubbery herbs were likely dried improperly or stored too long.

Next, decide how you want to rehydrate your herbs and spices. The traditional method is simply soaking them in warm water for a period of time. Use pure, filtered water and clean containers. Soak thick, dense herbs like rosemary or ginger up to 20 minutes. Delicate leafy herbs like parsley or cilantro may only need 5-10 minutes. Spices typically only require 5 minutes of soaking to fully rehydrate.

You can also choose to rehydrate herbs while cooking. Add dried leaves, seeds or powders at the start of simmering soups, stews or sauces. Over the cooking time, they will steadily rehydrate from the moisture in the dish. This infuses additional flavor throughout the entire recipe.

For quick use, cover dried herbs with boiling water and let sit for 1 minute. The hot water rapidly reconstitutes without over-soaking. Drain any excess liquid before adding herbs to uncooked foods like salads or dips where rehydration during cooking isn't possible.

Proper drainage and drying is key after rehydrating herbs by any soaking method. Shake off excess water and spread herbs on paper towels to absorb more moisture. Gently pat away residual dampness—rubbing can damage tender leaves. Allow 10-15 minutes for thorough draining before adding rehydrated herbs to recipes.

What about rehydrating salt-cured herbs and spices? Use boiling water rather than tepid; the heat helps draw out excess salts. Rinse rehydrated cured herbs under cool water before patting dry and using.

To enhance flavor, consider using vegetable or herb-infused oils, stocks or fruit juices instead of plain water for rehydrating. Soak basil in tomato juice before adding to pasta sauce. Rehydrate rosemary in leftover chicken broth for enhanced depth in soups or stews. Experiment with different liquids to complement the aroma of your specific herbs and spices.

Monitor the texture and color of rehydrated ingredients. Leaves and seeds should appear plump and vivid, while woody herbs and roots should feel supple, not brittle. Snip leaves from thicker stubs as needed. Discard any pieces that remain overly dry, shriveled or discolored after soaking.

Briefly sautéing or roasting rehydrated herbs before use helps intensify flavor. The heat releases essential oils that accumulate during storage. Just avoid overcooking delicate leaves.

Proper storage is important for rehydrated herbs, too. They are highly perishable so use within 3 days, keeping refrigerated. The compromised cell structure leads to faster spoilage after rehydration. Freeze leftovers in ice cube trays for longer storage.

With the right techniques, rehydrating and using your dried herbs, spices and roots can be simple and rewarding. Follow these tips for success:

- Select herbs dried and stored properly to maximize volatile oils.

- Soak in warm, filtered water 5-20 minutes depending on density.

- Drain, pat thoroughly dry, and allow to sit 10-15 minutes before using.

- Consider using flavorful liquids for more complex taste.

- Sauté or roast briefly to enhance intensity if desired.

- Use rehydrated herbs within 3 days and freeze extras for longer storage.

Rehydrating and using your dried herbs and spices helps minimize food waste while adding pronounced flavors to home cooking. With practice, you can masterfully resurrect your dehydrated ingredients into vivid, aromatic forms. Your food will practically pop with flavor and color.

CHAPTER 6

COOKING WITH DEHYDRATED FOODS

The Art of Rehydrating Foods

Bringing dehydrated foods back to life requires finesse. Mastering proper rehydration allows enjoying your dried ingredients at their best texture and flavor. Follow these techniques for expertly restoring fruits, vegetables, meats and herbs.

The goal is to fully reintroduce moisture without oversaturating. Use potable water, broths or natural juices to rehydrate. Start by submerging foods in room temperature liquid for 15-30 minutes. The amount of time depends on the food's density.

Fruits and veggies usually rehydrate within 15-20 minutes. Denser items like potatoes, corn, beans, meat chunks and thick fruits need 30-60 minutes soak time. Finely ground powders may take only 5-10 minutes to reconstitute.

To shorten rehydration time, use warm but not hot liquid. Heat speeds absorption but can cook delicate produce. Ideal soaking temperature is 110-120°F. You can also try a vacuum method, applying repeated pressure to force liquid into the food.

Check foods periodically, testing doneness by squeezing or taking a bite. Most fruits and veggies are done when pliable but not mushy. Meats should be flexible yet still firm. Stop soaking once the center is moist.

Drain away excess water after reconstituting to prevent diluted flavor and nutrients. Pat foods dry and finish by simmering, sautéing or roasting to blend flavors. Reserve soaking liquids for adding into sauces, soups or stews.

If using liquid other than plain water, factor in extra soaking time to allow seasoning integration. Dried beans, lentils and grains need 2-4 hours of soaking in salted broth to fully rehydrate.

Meats benefit from soaking in tomato, vegetable or meat broths. The savory essences penetrate deeply during rehydration. Fish can soak in citrus or wine-based liquids to impart flavors.

Fruits soak well in their own juices, diluted juices or liquors like rum, brandy, wine and kirschwasser. Extract maximum flavor by saving fruit dehydrating runoff for rehydrating that same fruit.

Herbs and garlic rehydrate quickly in minutes. Use warmer liquid for faster absorption. Alternatively, just crumble dried herbs into a dish as it cooks. The steam releases their essential oils and aromas.

Vegetable powders add concentrated nutrition to meals. Stir them into rice, pasta or soup broths as they cook. The heat and moisture seamlessly rehydrates them. Whisk into smoothies, hummus or dressings as well.

Minimize waste by reserving excess rehydration liquids for cooking. Strain them first if heavily flavored. Use soaking water from dried mushrooms or seafood to make amazing broths.

Troubleshooting tips:

- Cut dried food into smaller pieces to speed rehydration.

- If too dry after soaking, simmer in original liquid until fully restored.

- If product is mushy, use less soaking time and lower temperature liquid next time.

- For tacky fruit leathers, gently heat in the dehydrator to soften again.

With the right techniques, you can flawlessly rehydrate your dried ingredients for maximum enjoyment. Soon you will expertly revive fruits, vegetables, jerky and herbs to use in all your favorite recipes. Enjoy the convenience and nutrition of dehydrated foods thanks to your rehydration mastery.

Dehydrating during seasonal abundance allows enjoying produce year-round. Make big batches of dried fruits and vegetables when bountiful and cheap. With proper sanitation, pretreatment and storage, dried produce offers nutrients for over a year after harvest.

Preserve your garden's bounty at its peak flavor and nutrition. Halt ripening and degradation by quickly dehydrating abundant produce. Enjoy bright flavors and colors long after the growing season ends.

Reduce food waste by dehydrating leftovers and excess produce before it spoils. Powder older vegetables and fruits to add extra nutrition to meals. Dehydrate peels, stems and scraps for stock rather than trashing them.

Dehydration concentrates natural sugars and flavors. It intensifies tastes and unlocks unique textures. Incorporate rehydrated powders into juices, sauces, dressings and baked goods. Use dried mushrooms or tomatoes to add savory depth to soups, stews and casseroles.

With the rehydration guidance in this chapter, you can enjoy your dehydrated foods anytime. Revive them using the right techniques for optimal flavor, texture and nutrition. Let your creative cooking transform your pantry provisions into fabulous feasts all year long.

Incorporating Dehydrated Foods into Your Everyday Meals

Dehydrated ingredients lend convenience and big flavor to everyday home cooking. With a little creativity, dried fruits, vegetables, herbs, and meats can transform basic meals into hearty, nourishing fare for family and friends.

Soups and Stews

Rehydrate dried vegetables, beans, meat, and herbs by simmering in broth or water. Tomatoes, peppers, onions, carrots, peas, green beans, and potatoes all shine. Dried chopped chicken, beef, or ham make hearty additions. Dried herbs like basil, oregano, thyme, and parsley add depth.

Casseroles and Baked Dishes

Mix rehydrated vegetables like potatoes, broccoli, corn, spinach, and squash into casseroles. Add dried onions, mushrooms, tomatoes, and herbs. Top with crushed dried bread crumbs. Dried chopped chicken or tuna work well.

Salads and Sides

Toss dried fruits, chopped veggies, and herbs into greens and grain bowls. Cranberries, apples, tomatoes, onions, mushrooms, and bell peppers add color and crunch. Dried basil, thyme, parsley, dill lend fresh flavor.

Sandwiches and Wraps

Include dried tomato, onions, garlic, and diced meat in sandwich spreads. Layer on dried spinach, kale, peppers, and mushrooms. Shake on dried parsley, oregano, dill. Dried fruits add sweetness.

Pizza Toppings

Rehydrate diced sun-dried tomatoes, onions, garlic, and bell peppers in olive oil to spoon over pizza. Sprinkle on dried oregano, basil, rosemary, fennel.

Sauces, Spreads, and Dips

Puree dried tomatoes and peppers with oil and vinegar for an instant sauce. Blend dried herbs and spices into hummus, pesto, chutneys, and nut butters. Rehydrate mushrooms, onions, and garlic into creamy dips.

Bread and Baked Goods

Add dried fruits and spices to quick breads, muffins, and cakes. Use dried onions, garlic, and herbs in artisanal bread. Mix dried cranberries, cherries, apricots, or raisins into cookies and bars.

Breakfasts

Stir dried fruits into hot oatmeal and cereal. Add dried veggies to scrambled eggs and hash. Enjoy dried apple rings and mango on yogurt, ricotta, or cottage cheese. Shake cinnamon, nutmeg, and ginger into pancake batter.

With a well-stocked pantry of dried produce prepared in your dehydrator, quick yet creative meals utilizing these ingredients are always within reach.

Meal Ideas for Busy Parents

As a busy parent, it can be challenging to put wholesome, home-cooked meals on the table every night. When juggling kids, work, and activities, time is precious. However, with a bit of planning and some simple, fast recipes, you can provide nutritious dinners even on your busiest days. In this chapter, we'll explore kid-friendly meal ideas that come together quickly when you're crunched for time.

To start, take stock of any prepped ingredients you have on hand to build meals around. When you cook on less hectic days, double recipes and refrigerate or freeze half. Sauces, cooked grains, roasted vegetables, and shredded meats can all be batch prepped when you have more time. Having these ready-to-go ingredients cuts down prep work drastically on busy nights.

Another time-saving tip is to rely on foods that require little hands-on effort like slow cooker or one-pot meals. Toss ingredients into a crockpot in the morning or a sheet pan at night, and dinner practically cooks itself. Hearty chilis, stews, casseroles, and sheet pan bakes come together with minimal prep. You just assemble once and let the oven or slow cooker do the work.

Speaking of one-pan meals, also utilize skillet dinners as an easy weeknight solution. Quickly brown ground meat or chicken breast, then add rice, vegetables, and sauce right to the same pan. Stir fry ingredients or simmer a simple pasta dish all in one vessel to minimize clean-up.

When choosing recipes, opt for those with short ingredient lists you can shop for quickly. Skip complex dishes with rare spices or components. Simple combinations of protein, vegetables, starch, and sauce will satisfy kids and adults alike without the fuss.

Here are some specific, family-friendly 30-minute meal ideas requiring minimal prep:

- Baked salmon fillets with microwaved broccoli and instant rice or couscous

- Turkey or veggie burgers with sweet potato fries and carrot sticks

- Penne pasta with ready-made tomato sauce and meatballs or chickpeas

- Omelets with frozen chopped veggies and cheese shredded while eggs cook

- Bean and cheese quesadillas with homemade guacamole and salsa

- Chicken or shrimp fajitas wrapped in warmed whole wheat tortillas with fixings

- Pita pizzas made with pitas, jarred sauce, and favorite toppings

- Frittatas loaded with prepped veggies, cheese, and turkey sausage

- Chicken sausage links sliced into pasta tossed with olive oil, garlic, and spinach

- Grilled chicken breasts served with microwaved "steam in the bag" vegetables

The key is relying on ingredients that require little prep like pre-cooked proteins, frozen veggies, canned beans, quick-cooking grains, and ready-made sauces. Think low-fuss but highly nutritious.

With a well-stocked pantry, habit of batch prepping, and repertoire of streamlined recipes, you can feed your family wholesome dinners even when time is scarce. Don't sacrifice nutrition for convenience on hectic days. Lean on quick, nourishing meals that satisfy the group so you can all sit down together and enjoy some comfort and conversation at the end of a busy day.

Outdoor Recipes for Campers and Hikers

Enjoy nutritious, lightweight camp cuisine thanks to dehydrated ingredients. This chapter shares trail-friendly recipes to fuel outdoor adventures. Make tasty backpacking meals with just boiled water using your dried fruits, vegetables, meats, grains and seasonings.

Dried foods are perfect for packing since they are shelf-stable and extremely compact. They deliver concentrated calories and nutrition without extra weight or bulk. Rehydrating them with boiling water from a camp stove or fire is quick and easy.

Build hearty one-pot meals by combining dehydrated vegetables, meat chunks, seasonings and quick-cooking grains like quinoa, couscous or small pasta shapes. Boil for 10-15 minutes to rehydrate everything into a nourishing hot dinner.

Some favorite soup and stew combos include beef with carrots, onion and barley; chicken with sweet potatoes, kale and rice; lentil with tomatoes, peppers and pasta. Customize them to your taste.

For breakfast, make maple oatmeal by reconstituting quick oats and dried apples or blueberries with cinnamon, maple syrup powder and powdered milk or coconut milk powder. Prepare it at night and reheat in the morning.

Whip up fruit smoothies with powdered milk, dried banana slices, strawberries, mango or pineapple and protein powder. Just add water or milk and shake. Sprinkle with chia or flaxseeds for a nutrition and energy boost.

Craft hearty sandwiches on bagels, tortillas or pita bread. Fill them with tuna or salmon salad made with dried flakes, TVP-based vegan jerky with hummus, sun-dried tomato spreads or nut butters paired with dried fruit.

Snack on roasted seaweed sheets, banana chips, dried mango or pineapple rings, apple chips, veggie crackers, seed mixes enhanced with dried berries and yogurt-covered nuts or seeds. They provide quick energy.

Make single-serving just-add-water meals in zip-top bags. Combine couscous with dehydrated veggies, herbs and bouillon or rice noodles with coconut powder, spices, dried shrimp and vegetables.

For dessert, create instant pudding with dried fruit, sweetened condensed milk powder, vanilla powder and dessert gelatin or use cake and muffin mixes that only need water added.

Brew a warm campfire beverage like apple cider, spiced cider, cocoa or chai latte using your favorite dried fruits, chocolate powder, tea, spices and powdered milk.

With your dehydrator, you can custom-prepare tasty, nutritious ingredients for your next backpacking trip or family campout. Create meals you'll truly look forward to eating after a long day on the trail.

Dehydrating during abundant harvests allows enjoying produce year-round. Make big batches when fruits and vegetables are cheap and at their flavor and nutrition peak. With proper pretreatment and storage, dried produce offers nutrients for over a year after harvest.

Preserve your garden's bounty when ripe and fresh. Halt degradation and spoilage by quickly dehydrating extras as they come in. Enjoy intense flavors and colors long after the growing season ends.

Reduce food waste by dehydrating surplus garden produce before it spoils. Powder older vegetables and fruit to add concentrated nutrition into meals. Dehydrate all parts of plants - leaves, stems, peels, cores and seeds.

Dehydration condenses natural sugars and intensifies flavors. It unlocks unique textures perfect for packing. Incorporate rehydrated powders into trail drinks and meals. Use dried mushrooms, tomatoes or peppers to add interest to basic backpacking recipes.

With the tips in this chapter, you can craft flavorful camp cuisine using your dehydrated ingredients. Pack light and eat right with satisfying meals that rehydrate easily on the go. Enjoy nature's bounty harvested at its peak when you need it most out on the trail.

Emergency Meals for Preppers

When an emergency strikes, having a stockpile of dried and dehydrated foods can sustain you and your family. Plan shelf-stable rations to stay nourished in any situation that disrupts normal access to supplies.

Foundational Foods

Build your emergency food reserves around nutrient-dense staples with a long shelf life that provide calories and protein. Consider dried rice, beans, lentils, oats, wheat berries, cornmeal, and pasta. Dehydrate and store meats, eggs, dairy powder, nuts, and nut butters. Stock canned sardines, salmon, chicken, and tuna.

Dried Fruits and Vegetables

Home-dehydrated produce adds essential vitamins, minerals, and fiber. Prioritize potatoes, sweet potatoes, carrots, beets, onions, garlic, apples, oranges, berries, mushrooms, tomatoes, peppers, and greens. Supplement with commercially canned or pouched produce.

Fats and Oils

Healthy fats provide energy-dense calories and make food more palatable. Store oils with long shelf lives like olive and coconut oil. Other options: ghee, lard, tallow, nuts, nut butters, and seeds like flax, hemp, chia. Canned butter and cheese powder offer fat too.

Flavor Enhancers

Dried herbs, spices, bouillon, and sauces allow you to vary flavors and textures for morale. Grow and dry basil, oregano, cilantro, rosemary, thyme, and chili peppers. Stock curry powder, cumin, cinnamon, and chili powder. Add soy sauce, vinegar, hot sauce, and canned salsas.

Comfort Foods

Familiar favorites boost morale in stressful times. Consider storing instant mashed potatoes, dried pasta, rice mixes, pancake mix, powdered eggs, canned pie fillings, cookies, candy, and drink mixes like cocoa and tea.

Water

The essential prep - store at least 1 gallon per person daily. Reuse milk jugs and 2-liter bottles. Stock water purification tablets, filters, and bleach to disinfect found water sources if SHTF.

Emergency Meals

Combine foundational foods with dehydrated ingredients for well-rounded meals. Examples: rice and bean bowls with dehydrated veggies; potato soup with dried onions, carrots, greens; biscuits using dried eggs and evaporated milk; salmon cakes with dried potatoes.

By harnessing food dehydration, preppers can build resilient pantries allowing them to eat nutritiously for months when grocery stores are not an option.

.

CHAPTER 7

ADVANCED DEHYDRATION TECHNIQUES

Exploring Different Dehydration Methods

Dehydrating food as a preservation technique relies on removing moisture to inhibit bacterial growth and enzymatic reactions. But how that critical moisture removal is achieved can vary greatly depending on the dehydration method used. In this chapter, we'll provide an overview of common techniques from sun drying to oven drying and more modern methods.

The most traditional dehydration technique is open air sun drying. This involves spreading food items out on screens, trays or racks and relying on direct sunlight for moisture evaporation. Foods may be covered loosely with cheesecloth or netting to protect from insects. Sun drying is low-tech and requires no electricity, making it useful in remote regions. However, it is highly weather dependent and can be slow. Controlling precise temperatures and drying times is difficult.

Solar drying utilizes the sun's energy similar to open air drying but in an enclosed chamber. Foods sit on trays inside an insulated box with a clear top. The greenhouse effect heats and dries faster than open air sun while still protecting contents from pests. Solar driers can employ electric fans to enhance air circulation and speed drying times. This offers improved speed and control over purely passive sun drying.

Oven drying leverages the contained, controllable heat of kitchen appliances. Food items sit directly on oven racks or lined baking sheets with the oven set at 140-170°F. For added protection, screen drying racks placed above sheets can prevent scorching. Oven drying requires little specialized equipment but does demand more hands-on monitoring of internal temperatures and food doneness. Drying times vary based on oven accuracy and circulation.

Dehydrators provide customized temperature, airflow, and humidity control specifically for food drying. Specially designed models have stacked trays, heating elements, and a fan or exhaust system. This enables optimal conditions for safe, fast, efficient moisture removal. Dehydrators are easy to operate and Automated features can simplify the process greatly compared to more primitive drying methods. They yield consistent, high-quality results when used properly.

Freeze drying rapidly dehydrates food by freezing it first and then drawing off water vapor through reduced pressure conditions. As ice in the food turns from solid to gas, moisture evaporates without thawing. This sublimation process preserves textures and nutrition well but requires complex machinery. Freeze drying yields a high-quality finished product but with greater upfront costs.

Microwave drying leverages very short bursts of microwave energy to speed evaporation, though results can be uneven. Foods must be spread in thin layers and heated only briefly to avoid overcooking. Turntables and repeated stirring help distribute energy. While fast, microwave drying lacks fine process control and risks over-drying or cooking parts.

No matter which primary technique you choose, certain fundamentals remain constant. Sufficient airflow, careful regulation of temperature based on contents, and monitoring food doneness are vital to create stable, high-quality dehydrated foods. Match your drying method choice to your budget, location, and project goals for optimal results. With so many options available today, you're sure to find an effective dehydration technique for providing home-preserved foods your whole family can enjoy.

Dehydration for Gluten-Free and Low-Sodium Diets

Dehydration is a great way to create tasty, nutritious ingredients for special diets like gluten-free and low-sodium. Removing moisture naturally preserves foods without additives. With planning and care when selecting and preparing foods, your dehydrator can help you stick to your dietary needs.

Gluten is a protein found in grains like wheat, barley, rye and triticale. It provides elasticity to dough, but some people are sensitive or allergic. Look for labeled gluten-free grains like rice, corn, quinoa, amaranth, buckwheat and oats. Check seasonings too.

Fruits, vegetables, nuts, seeds, eggs, meat, poultry, fish and dairy are naturally gluten-free. Opt for produce in peak season from local farms when possible for best freshness and nutritional value.

Wash all produce thoroughly before dehydrating. Be diligent about avoiding cross-contamination when drying gluten-free and non-gluten-free foods. Use separate trays and utensils. Clean equipment thoroughly between use.

Make snacks like fruit leathers, veggie chips and dried fruit from fresh ingredients. Prepare broths using bones and certified gluten-free herbs and spices. Grind nuts into gluten-free flours.

Look for gluten-free pre-made products to dehydrate like pizza dough, pasta, waffles, crackers or batter mixes. Check labels to confirm no gluten sources. These make easy dried ingredients to reconstitute later.

Use corn or potato starch instead of wheat flour for dredging meats, thickening sauces or baking. Rinse dried starches thoroughly before consuming to remove any lingering traces of gluten proteins.

Breads, crackers and cereals are challenging without gluten. Use very thin slices, press wraps firmly onto trays and dry thoroughly on low heat to avoid crumbling.

Any homemade recipes can be adapted to be gluten-free by substituting alternate grains and flours. Adjust liquids and leaveners since gluten-free flours absorb differently. Expect denser results.

When rehydrating, use gluten-free broths, wines, vinegars and extracts to impart flavor. Check pre-made stocks andbouillons for gluten-containing ingredients. Use plain water if unsure.

Dehydration works well for low-sodium diets since no salt is required for preservation. Avoid adding salt during prep and marinating. Use herbs, spices, acids and sweeteners for flavor instead.

Fruits, vegetables and lean proteins are naturally lower in sodium. Opt for minimally processed items without added salt and rinse well before using.

Check prepared broths, stocks, bouillons and sauces for sodium content before using to rehydrate foods. Look for low-sodium varieties or dilute regular versions with water.

Add flavor without salt by using dried herbs, spices, onion, garlic and citrus zest. Blend your own unique seasonings. Marinate meats in oil, acids and sweeteners instead of salty brines.

With planning and care, dehydration can help you enjoy tasty, nutritious homemade foods that align with your dietary restrictions. Follow the tips in this chapter to create ingredients that suit your gluten-free and low-sodium needs.

Dehydrating in-season produce at its peak allows enjoying fruits and vegetables year-round. Make big batches when bountiful and cheap. With proper pretreatment and storage, dried produce offers nutrients for over a year after harvest.

Preserve your garden's ripe bounty before degradation occurs. Halt spoilage by quickly dehydrating abundant produce. Retain bright flavors and colors long after growing season ends.

Reduce waste by dehydrating extras and overripe produce before they spoil. Powder older vegetables and fruits to add concentrated nutrition into meals. Dehydrate all parts of plants including stems, leaves, peels and seeds.

Dehydration condenses natural sugars and intensifies flavors without added sodium or preservatives. It unlocks unique textures perfect for packing. Incorporate rehydrated powders into drinks, sauces and dishes for concentrated nutrition.

Follow this chapter's guidance to create flavorful, diet-appropriate ingredients. With planning and care, dehydration can help you stick to your gluten-free and low-sodium dietary needs while enjoying home-prepared, wholesome foods.

Creating Dehydrated Food Gifts and Crafts

Dehydrated fruits, vegetables, and herbs can become unique, personalized gifts from your kitchen. Get creative with homemade snacks, seasonings, and crafts using your dried bounty.

Fruit Leathers

Puree your favorite fruits into leathers. Roll up and wrap in waxed paper tied with raffia or baker's twine. Kids love these natural fruit "taffies" in fun shapes.

DIY Trail Mix

Trail mixes make great gifts for hikers. Combine dried fruits like mango, pineapple, banana, apricots, raisins, cranberries, apples, and citrus peels with nuts, seeds, coconut flakes, and optionally chocolate or yogurt drops. Package in reusable containers.

Herb and Spice Rubs

Create signature spice blends for meat and veggie rubs. Experiment with combinations of garlic, onion, paprika, cumin, coriander, mustard, pepper, cinnamon, cardamom, ginger, citrus zest. Jar and gift with recipes.

Herbal Tea Blends

Craft refreshing herbal tea blends using any dried herbs, fruits, and flowers from your garden. Lavender-lemon, chamomile-mint, hibiscus-berry — the options are endless. Package mixes in jars, sachets, or tea tins.

Simmering Spice Mixes

Put together warming mixes for cider, wine, wassail, or infused vinegars. Dried orange slices, cinnamon sticks, whole nutmeg, cloves, allspice, vanilla beans — tailor to the recipient's taste.

Dehydrated Soup and Sauce Mixes

Prepare customized all-in-one soup, sauce, and gravy mixes to which the recipient just adds water. You control the ingredients. Jar mixes with recipes.

Fruit and Nut Power Bars

Make chewy no-bake bars using dates, dried fruits, nuts, seeds, nut butters, puffed grains, shredded coconut and optional chocolate or carob chips. Wrap individually in waxed paper.

Scented Sachets

Fill cloth sachets with lavender buds, rose petals, lemon peel, vanilla beans, cinnamon sticks or mix botanicals. Tie with ribbon and tuck among linens, in dresser drawers, or closets to lightly scent.

Potpourri

Display dehydrated citrus slices, pine cones, flower petals, rose hips, star anise, allspice berries, and sticks in glass apothecary jars or bowls. Arrangements last for months.

The gift of homemade food and crafts using your dehydrator shows creativity and care. What everyday items will you transform?

Dehydrating for Long-Term Food Storage

Dehydrating is one of the most effective methods for long-term food storage and stockpiling emergency food reserves. Removing moisture preserves foods for 1-10+ years when done properly and stored in ideal conditions. In this chapter, we'll explore best practices for dehydrating food specifically with the goal of maximizing shelf life for long-term preparedness.

The keys to creating dehydrated foods that can be stored safely for years include: selecting optimal ingredients, employing pretreatments, achieving the right moisture content, pasteurizing after drying, proper cooling and conditioning, air-tight packaging, and climate controlled storage conditions.

Start by choosing ingredients known to dehydrate well and last long-term like beans, grains, powdered dairy, freeze dried produce, and lean proteins. Avoid ingredients prone to rancidity after dehydration such as nuts, whole eggs, and high fat meats. When using produce, opt for dried fruits and vegetables rather than fresh.

Use pretreatments like lemon juice, ascorbic acid, or sugar syrups to prevent browning and deterioration in certain fruits and veggies. These inhibit oxidation and enzyme reactions during the drying process. For added protection, you can also blanch produce prior to dehydrating.

Monitor foods closely during dehydration and test doneness to achieve optimal moisture levels below 10-15%. Use a refractometer to scientifically measure water activity. Meat jerky should have a flexible leathery texture without moisture pockets. Fruits and veggies should be crisp and brittle.

After dehydrating, pasteurize all foods by heating at 160-170°F for 15-30 minutes to destroy any remaining microbial contaminants. Then cool and condition the dried goods for 1-2 weeks in sealed containers out of light. This allows moisture to equalize and textures to stabilize.

Package dried foods in moisture-proof containers like glass jars, Mylar bags, or vacuum seal pouches. Oxygen absorbers and desiccants can help remove any trace air and moisture. Store containers in a cool, dry, dark place like a basement or cellar with consistent temperatures around 60°F and 35% humidity. Refrigeration or freezing extends shelf life even further.

Here are some specific ingredients and tips to maximize dehydrated food longevity:

- White rice, beans, oats, pasta: Dehydrate until brittle with no moisture pockets. Store in Mylar with oxygen absorbers.

- Dairy powder: Choose low-fat versions and dehydrate into powder. Can last 20+ years.

- Freeze dried produce: Handles long-term storage well compared to air dried fruits and veggies.

- Meat: Use very lean meats. Dehydrate into jerky with 10% moisture content. Refrigerate or freeze for best life.

- Fats: opt for oils rather than solid fats. Store in oxygen-free dark bottles in the refrigerator.

With the right ingredients and effective techniques, dehydrating food can yield nutritious, tasty options for your long-term stockpile. Follow best practices from start to finish, and your dried goods can nourish your family for years to come in an emergency situation. Peace of mind comes from knowing you have a stable food supply in order to be prepared for whatever the future holds.

Tips for Maximizing the Shelf Life of Dehydrated Foods

Getting the longest shelf life from dehydrated foods requires careful handling and storage. Follow these guidelines to retain optimal quality and safety for months or years after drying.

Start with peak quality ingredients free of bruises, damage or spoilage. Wash produce thoroughly before dehydrating. Keep appliances and surfaces sanitized to avoid contamination.

Pre-treat foods properly before dehydrating for maximum shelf stability. Blanch or steam vegetables to halt ripening enzymes. Acidify fruits. Partially cook or freeze dense veggies and meats.

Dry foods quickly at optimal temperatures - 130-140°F for fruits, vegetables and herbs, 160°F for meats and fish. Higher heat helps destroy microbes and enzymes causing deterioration.

Monitor closely and rotate trays periodically for consistent drying. Discard any pieces that appear spoiled. Check for doneness to prevent over-drying. Condition properly after dehydrating.

Test dried foods to confirm they contain little remaining moisture. Fruits and veggies should have no moist pockets and be leathery or brittle. Meats should be firm with no visible moisture.

For long-term storage, pasteurize conditioned dried foods to destroy any remaining microbial spores. Place foods in 175°F oven for 15 minutes or freeze below 0°F for a few days.

Package dried foods in moisture-proof containers like mason jars, vacuum seal pouches or freezer bags. Oxygen absorbers and desiccants prolong quality.

Label containers with contents and date before sealing. Store in a cool, dark, dry place around 60°F. Refrigeration or freezing gives maximum shelf life.

Check periodically for signs of spoilage like mold, yeast growth, condensation, sliminess, off odors or change in texture or appearance. Discard any deteriorated foods.

Rehydrate dried foods using clean potable water. Discard used liquid after and avoid cross-contamination with utensils. Cook rehydrated meats, fish and vegetables thoroughly before consuming.

Shelf life varies based on multiple factors:

- Fruits/Veggies - 6-12 months shelf; 1 year refrigerated; 2 years frozen

- Meats/Fish - 1 year shelf; 2 years refrigerated; 3+ years frozen

- Herbs/Spices - 1-3 years shelf; 4 years refrigerated

Key Tips:

- Start with peak quality ingredients

- Follow proper pretreatment, dehydration and conditioning steps

- Use moisture-proof packaging and oxygen absorbers

- Label containers with contents and date

- Store in cool, dark location around 60°F

- Refrigerate or freeze for extended shelf life

- Check periodically for signs of spoilage

- Discard deteriorated or expired foods

By following best practices from start to finish, you can maximize the usable shelf life of your home dehydrated foods. Take steps to optimally process, package and store items. With care, your nutritious homemade ingredients will retain excellent quality for many seasons of enjoyment.

Dehydrating surplus produce allows enjoying nutrients year-round. Make big batches when fruits and vegetables are abundant and cheap. With proper sanitation, pretreatment and storage, dried foods offer flavors and nutrition for over a year after harvest.

Preserve your garden's ripe bounty before degradation occurs. Halt spoilage by quickly dehydrating extras following best practices. Enjoy intense flavors and bright colors long after growing season ends.

Reduce food waste by dehydrating leftovers and excess produce before they spoil. Powder older vegetables and fruits to add concentrated nutrition into meals. Dehydrate all parts of plants including stems, leaves, peels and seeds.

Dehydration condenses natural sugars and flavors without preservatives or additives. It unlocks unique preserved textures perfect for portable snacks, camping meals and pantry stocking.

Using this chapter's guidance, you can maximize shelf life for all your dehydrated foods. Follow each step carefully from ingredient selection through storage. With diligent technique, you can enjoy home-dried produce for many future seasons.

BONUS 1

RAW FOOD RECIPES - 15 TUTORIALS

Scan the QR Code

BONUS 2

33 TUTORIAL RECIPES

Scan the QR Code

BONUS 3

21 FOODS TUTORIALS

Scan the QR Code

EXCLUSIVE BONUS

3 EBOOK

Scan the QR code or click the link and access the bonuses

http://subscribepage.io/01tYl3

Hector Rend

Hector Rend is a renowned and influential author in the field of cooking and the art of food dehydration. With extensive experience in the field, he has devoted much of his life to researching, experimenting and sharing knowledge on food dehydration techniques.

From a young age, Hector has cultivated a passion for cooking and the art of food preservation. He has spent years studying different dehydration methodologies, testing his skills and learning from experts in the field.

In addition to his career as an author, Hector has spent many years traveling to explore different culinary traditions and food dehydration techniques around the world. These experiences enrich his perspective and make him an expert who can offer a comprehensive approach to food dehydration.

Hector Rend continues to dedicate himself to his passion for the culinary arts and food dehydration. His life is a continuous journey of discovery and sharing authoritative information in the field. Through his work, he inspires culinary enthusiasts around the world to explore new horizons and experiment with food dehydration to create delicious and healthy dishes.

Made in United States
Troutdale, OR
12/26/2023